England *v.* West Indies 1981

The Official England Team Tour Book

Edited by PETER SMITH

PELHAM BOOKS

First published in Great Britain by
Pelham Books Ltd
44 Bedford Square
London WC1B 3DU
1981

British Library Cataloguing in Publication Data

England v. West Indies 1981.
1. Cricket — West Indies — History
I. Smith, Peter
796.35'865 GV928.W47

ISBN 0 7207 1353 6

Typeset by Cambrian Typesetters
Farnborough, Hampshire

Printed and bound by Billings, Guildford and Worcester

Contents

Foreword by Alec Bedser 7
1 Ian Botham — Answering the critics 9
2 Brian Rose — Introduction to the Caribbean 19
3 Graham Stevenson — St Vincent and one day international 34
4 Peter Willey — England in Trinidad 49
5 Paul Downton — My Test debut in Trinidad 60
6 Bob Willis — Returning home 74
7 Geoff Miller — Taking over the vice-captaincy 81
8 David Bairstow — Second one day international 89
9 Robin Jackman & Alan Smith — The 'Jackman Affair' 99
10 Bill Athey — Flying in from Australia 115
11 Roland Butcher — Back home in Barbados 120
12 Graham Gooch — My Test century in Barbados 133
13 Chris Old — Playing in Montserrat 146
14 John Emburey — Fourth Test in Antigua 153
15 Graham Dilley — Fast bowling overseas 165
16 Mike Gatting — My comeback in Jamaica 171
17 David Gower — Coming of age in final Test 179
Test averages 192

Publisher's note: It had been hoped to include in this book a chapter by Geoffrey Boycott, but this has not been possible since he has been for some time under exclusive contract to his own publishers.

CREDIT

All the photographs are reproduced by permission of the photographer Adrian Murrell of Allsport Photographic.

England *v.* West Indies 1981 Principal Dates

Jan. 15	Team left London and arrived in Antigua for five day acclimatisation period.
Jan. 26	Beat Young West Indies XI by 190 runs in opening four day fixture at Pointe-a-Pierre, Trinidad.
Feb. 1	Bob Willis injures knee in one day fixture against Windward Islands in St Vincent.
Feb. 4	Lost to West Indies by two runs in first one day international in St Vincent.
Feb. 10	Drew with Trinidad and Tobago in four day match in Port of Spain.
Feb. 13	Start of first Test match in Port of Spain delayed for three hours because of wicket repairs following damage inflicted by overnight saboteur protesting at absence of Trinidad wicket-keeper and captain Deryck Murray from West Indies side. Small section of crowd hurl bottles on to outfield angry at delayed start.
Feb. 18	Lost to West Indies by innings and 79 runs in first Test in Port of Spain, Trinidad.
Feb. 19	Bob Willis, vice-captain, advised to return home for treatment to knee injury. Robin Jackman (Surrey) sent for as replacement.
Feb. 22	Geoff Miller (Derbyshire) confirmed as new tour vice-captain.
Feb. 23	Jackman flew into Guyana. Political writer in Jamaica called for Jackman to be banned because of his 'South African connections'.
Feb. 24	First indication given to manager Alan Smith that Jackman's South African connections being questioned by Guyanese Government.
Feb. 25	Brian Rose discovered to have eye defect and decision taken for him to return home immediately.

Feb. 26	Lost to West Indies by six wickets in second one day international in Berbice. Jackman served with deportation order on his return with team from Berbice to Georgetown, Guyana. Second Test in Guyana cancelled when Cricket Council object to Guyana Government interfering with make up of tour party.
Feb. 27	England team leave Guyana to take up temporary residence in Barbados.
Mar. 1	Foreign Office officials from Barbados, Montserrat, Antigua and Jamaica start meeting in secret hotel hideout to decide whether tour should be allowed to continue with Jackman an acceptable member of party.
Mar. 4	Announced at one am that tour would be allowed to continue as scheduled without any restrictions.
Mar. 6	Bill Athey (Yorkshire) flew in from Sydney, Australia as replacement for Brian Rose.
Mar. 10	Drew with Barbados in four day match.
Mar. 12	Jackman selected for first Test cap along with West Indian born Roland Butcher.
Mar. 14	Ken Barrington, tour assistant manager, died following heart attack in hotel bedroom.
Mar. 18	Lost to West Indies by 298 runs in third Test in Barbados.
Mar. 24	Beat Leeward Islands by five wickets in four day match in Montserrat.
Apr. 1	Draw with West Indies in fourth Test in Antigua.
Apr. 7	Draw with Jamaica in four day match in Kingston.
Apr. 15	Draw with West Indies in fifth Test in Kingston, Jamaica.
Apr. 17	Depart Jamaica for London.

Foreword

Alec Bedser
(Chairman of England's Selectors)

We knew it was going to be a tough assignment for the players when we sat down to pick the tour party. We had all seen the strength of the West Indies side at home during the previous few months. The winter before they had outclassed Australia in Australia. Now they would be playing at home with all the advantages that brings with it, keen to show off to their own public exactly why they were regarded as the best team in the world at both the five day Test match level and one day internationals.

Really it was not a mission for young players — particularly batsmen — who were relatively inexperienced in playing Test cricket. This was our biggest problem when we sat down in September, 1980. There were perhaps half a dozen players, all vastly experienced, who would have been the first under discussion in normal circumstances. Unfortunately they were never mentioned for one reason or another.

There was Mike Brearley who had announced during the tour of Australia the previous winter that he would not be available for any more tours. If he had, I've no doubt he would have continued his captaincy reign but his decision forced us to turn to somebody else for the 1980 series at home. We decided to give Ian Botham his chance in the knowledge that he lacked leadership experience but confident that he would learn as he went along and would provide England with a long term solution.

Half way through the 1980 series Alan Knott informed us that he was not available for the West Indies tour. His Kent colleague Derek Underwood indicated to us that he was not keen to go because he would have liked a winter at home after all the touring he has done over the years. Phil Edmonds, another left arm spinner, was still handicapped by the after effects of a knee operation when the tour side was chosen and Mike Hendrick informed us he did not wish to be considered.

There were five players, all very experienced tourists, with almost three hundred Test caps between them who were not available. Two or three of them would have helped give us a better balance between experienced players and the younger ones on the tour. That balance was not helped when Bob Willis, the vice captain, had to return home without being able to play in a Test match and was soon followed by Brian Rose after the first Test. With all his touring experience Willis was obviously a key selection and Rose's eye defect robbed the side of a left handed batsman.

When taking all these difficulties into account and the many setbacks the touring party suffered during the opening month of the tour, it was probably surprising so much emerged on the credit side to help England build a side for the future. There were quite a number of credits.

Take Graham Gooch who has now matured and become a true Test batsman scoring the runs he should do at that level. The advancement of David Gower is another plus. He has perhaps been a little unfortunate in being tossed into Test cricket before he was ready. At his present age he should only just be on the fringe of Test selection but, lacking class-looking batsmen as we have done in the past, he was given a chance before he had really established himself as a county cricketer. The winter in the Caribbean has now taught him what playing Test cricket is all about and England should benefit in the future.

Three or four other players went there before they could be classified as true Test players. Mike Gatting, Bill Athey and Graham Stevenson are all at the apprenticeship stage and the going was hard for them but we are hoping they have learned considerably from the experience and will be capable of challenging for a regular place in the near future.

The party may have lost the series two nil which is a better record than many people predicted but English Test cricket should prove to be healthier for the experience.

1 IAN BOTHAM (ENGLAND CAPTAIN & SOMERSET)

The England captain gives his impressions of the tour and answers his critics.

I was a proud and happy man when I first set foot in the West Indies last January despite a record of one defeat and not a single victory in my six Test match reign as England captain. Three months later I left the West Indies still searching for my first win as England's Test match leader. The record of defeats under my command had trebled to three. Yet I led the team out of Jamaica even more proud and happy — and with my head held high.

We were a beaten side, certainly. Outplayed in the first two Test matches. But I believe we left the Caribbean richer for all that, a much better side than when we started and only two or three players away from being a very good one again. We had nothing to feel ashamed about.

There was the emergence of Graham Gooch as a century hitting opening batsman to form with Geoff Boycott a partnership which proved more effective than that of Gordon Greenidge and Desmond Haynes who were accepted as the best opening pair before the tour started. There was the confirmation that David Gower has now found his feet at a Test match level ready to take his place in the rich line of number four batsmen England have produced over the years. There was the satisfaction of seeing John Emburey establish himself as the most effective off spinner in Test cricket today, the growing strength of Graham Dilley as a fast bowler who will soon become as consistently fast as anybody in the world, the courage of Peter Willey which inspired us all and the rapid development of Paul Downton to the stage where he finished the tour looking as though he belonged behind the wicket at a Test level.

Six players who returned home better equipped to serve England at a Test level in the future than they had been at the start of the year. And this from a tour that far more experienced travellers than I have described as the hardest and most distressing they had ever known as a result of all the off the field disasters which caused us to stumble during the first six weeks of the visit.

There was a seventh who came back better equipped to do the job he had been commissioned to do; myself. As a captain I readily admit that I went out there short of leadership experience, lacking in tactical knowledge. I was well aware of my own shortcomings. When I was first appointed at the start of the 1980 summer at home, I realised that it would take me at least two series before I really knew what it was all about and before I could be considered alongside some of the great names who have had the role before me.

I was well aware too, that long before the tour was over, demands were being made for my head. Yet I believe I returned two thirds if not three quarters of the way to being the man and captain capable of holding down the most demanding position in English sport.

I made mistakes, of course. But I hope and believe I learned from every one of them. If I could replay the whole tour over again, I would do some things differently. But that is part of the whole process of growing up, picking up knowledge and advice as you go and preparing for the future.

Anyone who expected me to take over against the acknowledged champions of cricket in both the one day and five day game and lead a largely inexperienced side to victory by emerging as a complete master of all I controlled must have been crazy. I don't think anybody seriously expected us to win the series. The forecast of most experts before we left was that we were headed for defeat in all five Test matches. We did better than that, and against all the odds.

Let us put the whole thing into perspective. We were taking on a side with the best fast attack cricket has known. Not just two outstanding quick bowlers who have generally proved sufficient in cricket history to make their international side the leading Test playing country of the day. But four outstanding quick bowlers superbly deployed by Clive Lloyd who have destroyed every side they have met over the previous four years. If the tour had gone without a single hitch we would have been constantly up against it, fighting for survival against the relentless pounding of constant pace at an over rate which doesn't allow the opposition to build match winning scores fast enough even if the batsmen can survive.

But there were hitches, each one of which could have blown the tour apart. They came rolling along, one almost overtaking the other, building up like a giant snowball tumbling out of control down a hill and trying to sweep aside everything in its path. You have to be unlucky to go to the Caribbean in its dry season and find monsoon like rain washing out matches and vital practice sessions early in the tour — practice sessions we desperately needed after a four month break immediately following our domestic programme at home.

Then there was the tragic loss of both Bob Willis and Brian Rose, two of the most experienced players in the party who were expected to fill key positions in the side. The return home of Bob after bowling less than eight overs on the tour meant that my initial fire power planned for the Test series was cut by half as well as missing a man whose advice I valued. We had only just recovered from the shock of losing him through a knee injury when we learned that Brian would have to leave too because of an eye defect. In less than a week I had been robbed of one of my main strike bowlers and my number three batsman, one who had performed so heroically against the same West Indies fast bowlers in England in helping to give the side the start it needed.

Within hours of learning of Brian's troubles came the political interference over Robin Jackman's addition to the tour party, the cancellation of the second Test in Guyana, the flight to freedom from Georgetown and the days in Barbados when nobody could settle, living from hour to hour wondering whether we might be bustled on another jet and flown home.

Finally came the greatest tragedy of all with the loss of Ken Barrington following a heart attack at the end of the second day of the third Test in Barbados. Ken was more than an assistant manager. He was a friend, a pal, a father to us all who understood the individual needs of every player on the party. You had to be a member of the party to realise how much he meant to us all and surely no other captain in cricket history has led a side out on the field knowing that eight or nine of the men behind him were openly crying. There were tears in my eyes too and it was a good ten minutes before most of us could focus properly, eyes drying in the need to perform to the standard Ken would have wanted.

By the time the series of disasters had come to an end, we were two down in the Test series itself. The outlook was depressing. The threat of a complete whitewash, a record of four defeats out of four plus two others in the one day internationals. How else could I have returned home but a proud and happy man for the way the team pulled together behind me, rallied around and emerged from the final two Tests in Antigua and Jamaica with credit. That took character and guts.

The most frequent charge levelled at me throughout the series — and even before the tour started — was one of being naïve. I was mocked because I said we stood a chance of winning the series before we left England. But what did people expect me to say as England's leader? That we stood no chance. It may have been nearer the truth but I've never been one to accept defeat or even think in terms of defeat until the match has been lost.

On every rest day of the four Test matches we found ourselves in a position where we were fighting to save the game. The first question asked at the traditional rest day Press Conference was always 'Can we save it?' My answer was always the same 'Of course we can' for which I was taken to task when we lost in Trinidad and Barbados. But again what else could I have said as England's leader? I had to believe we can to help give the rest of the players confidence. If I did not think we stood a chance and said so openly, how could I expect them to give everything in staging a rearguard action?

I did believe it too even if the critics did not. I had more faith in the men with me than most others, a faith justified by the way we clawed our way out of deep trouble both in Antigua and Jamaica when Clive Lloyd was saying he had the fire power on worn wickets to win.

The greatest complaint about my whole tour performance was that I could not handle the strain of leading the side and perform to my own ability as a player. That the whole double role of having to think for others and thinking for myself was too much and I had deteriorated to a stage as a player where I was hardly worth a place in the side. I reject such charges completely.

I know the figures may not support my case. In twenty-five Test innings before I took over the England captaincy I had scored six centuries. Since being leader I had managed only one half century and that in the first Test as captain at Trent Bridge in the 1980 summer. My test record in the West Indies read a depressing 0; 16; 26; 1; 13 and 16 for a total of 73 runs from seven innings. Before assuming the captaincy I had also taken five or more wickets in a Test innings fourteen times, something I have not managed to do since.

Let me say straight away that I was extremely disappointed in my run return. Let me also put the record straight by saying that not once did I find the leadership a strain or feel that it was affecting my form. In fact I enjoyed the captaincy.

In my own defence I would point out that I took fifteen West Indies wickets which was five more than the next most successful bowler Graham Dilley despite having to turn myself into a new ball bowler as well as a stock bowler following the return home of Bob Willis. I bowled more overs on the tour than I might have done if Bob had been able to stay with us.

Of course I probably took more out of myself than I expected. In normal circumstances that would not have mattered but against the West Indies it did. Even allowing for the good starts Geoff Boycott and Graham Gooch gave us in several innings, I generally found myself with my pads on preparing to go in within a couple of hours of our innings starting. There was no time to rest, put my feet up and prepare myself mentally for batting as there had been in the past when I was making those centuries. Those conditions would have been the same whether I was captain or not.

No, leading the side did not impose any extra strain or affect my performance. One of the great enjoyments of the tour was breaking new frontiers as a leader, thinking about the game more than I had ever done in the past, discovering a new rhythm and approach.

Captaincy provided me with an experience I had never

come across before, that of man management. You only flirt with it at home when you have the players together for just six days at a time. On tour when you become a sixteen strong family for three months at a time, man management plays such an important factor. It was the hardest part of the captaincy role, one I believed I got better at as the tour went on. Despite all the setbacks and interruptions, the morale and team spirit remained high right until the end.

As a captain you feel much more for the players around you than you do when just a member of the side. You feel for them in their moments of disappointment, share with them their moments of delight. I was very glad, for instance, that I was at the wicket when David Gower reached his century in the second innings of the final Test in Jamaica. Knowing how hard David had worked to make himself into a Test batsman equipped to hold down the number four position, I wanted to be the first to shake him by the hand after reaching the magic figure which confirmed his class.

Graham Gooch could not have been more delighted than I was when he reached his century against the West Indies in the second innings in Barbados and the first innings in Jamaica. I felt delighted for John Emburey when he took five wickets in the West Indies innings in Trinidad. And nobody could have felt more sorry when I blundered in attempting to take a slip catch in Jamaica which would have given Graham Dilley a wicket he greatly deserved at the time.

Sharing the joy of the others around you provided some of the high spots of the tour. There were a few low spots as well. Getting out in the second innings of the first Test in Trinidad when we were just three hours from safety was the lowest spot of all. Not getting out, but the way I fell.

It was a stroke condemned by everybody who saw it when I attempted to hit Viv Richards over the top but skied the ball into the hands of Michael Holding instead at deep mid-off. The new ball was only four overs or so away and I should have been there with Geoff Boycott to greet it and protect the batsmen to come. As soon as I saw the ball nestle into Holdings' hands, I knew it would make headline news back home. It was so frustrating.

Of course I regret getting out that way. Yet I'm not entirely convinced it was such a bad stroke to attempt and I still wonder what the reaction would have been if the ball had carried as I intended and gone over the boundary for six. The pressure was building up at the time, Clive Lloyd was crowding the bat, the ball was tossed up and everything was right for me to have a go and attempt to relieve a little of the pressure. The crime was not having a go as I did. My crime was failing to connect properly.

I've wondered since whether I would have been so thoroughly condemned if I had not been captain. It has been because I've taken such risks in similar, tight circumstances that I've been praised in the past, heralded as a batsman with a bright, new outlook on the game who was prepared to take the fight to the enemy. That's the way I've always played it.

Generally it's been the right way to play it too. There's been too much rubbish written and talked about applying the right technical and tactical approach to given situations. For years the West Indian batsmen have been held up as shining examples of how to do the unorthodox and get away with it and I've longed to see more of their approach in English cricket — somebody willing to go out and hit the ball even if they haven't been technically correct on the point of contact.

Apply it to golf where so much is talked about style. There is no point in possessing a swing like Tom Watson, the putting touch of Jack Nicklaus of old if you are going to hit the ball with all the might of a Pansy Potter. Nobody will win anything at golf that way or be worth watching. Give me a Severiano Ballesteros everytime.

If the West Indies had batted as many expect English players to bat all the time, we might have been more successful on the tour. Twice we had chances of making a first innings breakthrough against the West Indies in the Test series. Once when they were 65 for four in Barbados and again when they were 179 for three — still 106 runs behind — in Jamaica. On each occasion Clive Lloyd promoted himself one place up the West Indies batting order and got them out of trouble. Not by defending solidly but standing up straight and boldly carrying the fight back to us with a series of flashing strokes, most of them risky in their execution but all risk forgotten or ignored when the ball crashed against the boundary board. It was the method Graham Gooch adopted when he was in trouble against Colin Croft in his Test century in Jamaica. In two overs he was in so much trouble he could have been excused for going into his shell. Instead he took Croft on with such telling effect that the bowler who had caused us such agony and despair during the first three Test matches had to be withdrawn from the firing line having given away 33 runs off four overs.

Mentioning Clive Lloyd, I would like to thank him and his players for the spirit in which the tour was conducted. Any Test series involving a fast attack such as the one they possessed has a high element of risk about it where the feelings of players can boil over — batsmen on the receiving end of short, intimidatory bowling fighting for their lives . . . bowlers who are known to have short fuses and can let their feelings run away if they don't get decisions in their favour.

Although I felt that once or twice they rather overdid the short stuff against our tail end batsmen, there was no nastiness throughout the series. Undoubtedly my own personal relationship with Viv Richards and Clive helped, the rest of the side worked hard at reaching a good understanding with the opposition and they responded in a similar way.

I'm convinced — and so is Clive — this was the basic reason why it was the most trouble free — spectatorwise — tour there has been to the West Indies in modern times. No riots, no stoning, no stands burned down, no hold-ups. Not once could the crowds who filled the grounds on the first three days of the last three Test matches in Barbados, Antigua and Jamaica, take exception to anything that went on from a cricket playing point of view.

On the whole the crowds were marvellous. Only in Port of Spain, Trinidad did we encounter any degree of hostility and that was caused, in the main, by the non selection of Trinidad captain Deryck Murray in the Test side and a remarkable reluctance on the part of the ground authority to explain the true causes for the delayed start on the first day.

The sun was shining brightly, the umpires made several wicket inspections, the ground looked perfectly playable from the boundary edge yet little or no attempt was made to inform the spectators that play was not possible because of damp patches on the wicket itself where it had been repaired following the work of an overnight intruder and a large boggy area behind one wicket as a result of a leaking tap in the ground water system.

Understandably the crowd grew more and more restless as the hours ticked by. The only information they were fed over the loudspeaker system was the timing of the next inspection. Both Clive and I, plus the umpires Clyde Cumberbatch and Douglas Sang Hue were in complete agreement that the match should not start until the conditions were fair for both batsmen and bowlers alike. Clive and I still felt that way when we were ordered to start play with the authorities growing more and more concerned about possible crowd reaction if the match did not get underway almost immediately.

When we went out to toss up, a small section of the crowd at the far end of the ground let their frustrations show by throwing a few bottles and cans on the outfield. It was well away from us but Clive was all for turning back until I persuaded him such action might inflame a delicate situation.

That wicket was still not right when we started and I was disappointed in the wickets we found throughout the islands. There was far too much grass on the wicket in Barbados and most of the others produced uneven bounce. I was upset, too, in the lack of practice facilities offered to us. Most of the pitches were unsuitable, poorly prepared and protected although the ground authorities in each case did have a partial excuse in the unseasonable rain. The covers available on the majority of Test grounds were sparse and out of date.

It was upsetting when taking into consideration the lengths to which we in England go towards providing the best of cricketing facilities for touring sides, ensuring that Test match wickets are fair to both sides despite our uncertain weather. When we travel overseas we have come to expect that the Test match wickets will favour the home side and I do not believe we make the fuss we should do when things are not right.

In order to ensure more uniformity of conditions the International Cricket Conference has started a system of sending independent observers to Test matches to report on the conduct of matches, player's living accommodation, dressing room facilities etc. For three Tests in the West Indies former Pakistan Test captain and leg spinner Intikhab Alam was on the scene, the first time England had been involved in a series with an observer present.

The idea is sound. However I urge the International Cricket Conference to give these observers stronger and wider powers if the scheme is to be completely successful and cricket is to be played in the best possible conditions throughout the world.

Despite the few hassles, the disasters, the disappointments, I'd like to emphasise again I enjoyed the experience of leading England overseas. To manager Alan Smith, a figure of comfort throughout the tour, to physiotherapist Bernard Thomas who again performed wonders on the treatment table and was such a tremendous help to us all following the loss of Kenny and to all the players who came through the campaign smiling whether they made the Test side or not, I'd like to say a very sincere thank you for their support. I hope I am given the opportunity of leading England overseas again.

2 BRIAN ROSE (SOMERSET & ENGLAND)

President's Young West Indies XI *v.* England
23–26 January

Brian Rose tells of his first impressions of the Caribbean and of adjusting to the slower pace of life. He describes the practice period in Antigua and the first game of the tour in Trinidad.

One of the joys of touring, I understood, was finding a never ending stream of good, firm wickets underfoot, sun on your back, smooth, flat and hard outfields where a stroke perfectly timed sent the ball racing to the boundary with just the merest hint of persuasion. My romance with the Caribbean scene lasted just three balls; on a wet wicket at that. The type I could find back at home from Taunton to Scarborough without having to cross the Atlantic.

There was Malcolm Marshall of Hampshire, Barbados and the West Indies rushing in. A fuller length delivery than the previous two he had sent my way. I went forward, confident I had it well covered when it bounced a little more than I expected off the damp turf and silly mid-off had no difficulty accepting the chance that came his way.

As I turned back to the pavilion at Guaracara Park situated on the edge of the giant Texaco oil refinery at Pointe-a-Pierre some forty miles from Port of Spain, Trinidad, I couldn't help thinking back to the first and only previous time I had toured abroad with England — to Pakistan in 1977 under Mike Brearley's captaincy. The wicket there was damp for the first match in Rawalpindi. And scarred too, in places, where barbed wire had been dragged across it that first morning as workmen hurriedly erected fences at the last moment to keep the crowd out. I was out for a duck there, left facing a pair in the opening match. History was repeating itself four years later when England's selectors had given me a second chance. I couldn't have felt more miserable.

It was in complete contrast to the way I had felt that morning on the forty mile drive to the ground with us all packed into a mini-bus, supposedly air conditioned. The only way we could air condition it was to open all the windows and catch a breeze to relieve the heat of a typical West Indian day. I thought then on the hour long journey how well things had gone for me in particular and the team in general on our introduction to the Caribbean.

I was really the new boy on the party. Everybody else from manager Alan Smith downwards had been to the Caribbean before in one way or another. They had either been on previous England tours like Geoff Boycott, Chris Old and Bob Willis, on private cricketing tours or on holiday. I had never previously set foot in that part of the world. It lived up to everything I had been led to expect, particularly the first five days in Antigua, one of the most popular islands in the Leeward range. The home, of course, of my Somerset colleague and West Indies super batsman Viv Richards.

Back in December I had been pounding my way along the beach at Weston-super-Mare where I live on daily two mile running stints building up my fitness for the tour. I had not once glanced at the sea. Walk a few minutes along the fine, sandy beaches of Antigua and it is hard to resist throwing yourself into the water time and time again. It is so warm, calm, blue and inviting — better than any swimming pool.

The five day acclimatisation programme was essential. Without it I think we would have been in trouble from the start. The official West Indies tour programme had launched us into the opening four day match against the President's Young West Indies XI within two days of our arrival. I can appreciate their financial difficulties which force them to keep the length of the tour down to a bare minimum but it is unfair to expect any player to come from the cold of an English winter not having played cricket for four months and pick up the game as though there had been no break at all.

The first five days were financed by the Test and County Cricket Board and they proved a wise investment especially to someone like me. A hamstring injury in the final Test against the West Indies at Headingley last August had put me out of cricket for a while. Then I received a cracked rib in

Somerset's final John Player League match of the summer which took time to heal. I had spent a considerable time running to build up my fitness and stamina and also visited the indoor school at Taunton for practices. Arriving in Antigua I still felt I needed to feel that special touch of ball on bat before I was ready to play an innings in the middle.

Although the whole thing was a new adventure for me I don't think I have seen anybody more excited on the outward journey than Roland Butcher, born and raised in his early years in Barbados, now happily settled in London playing for Middlesex and making history as the first true West Indian to be selected for an England touring party. The highlight was just after we took off from Barbados on the second leg of the journey out from Heathrow. On the first leg the plane had been almost half empty which meant that we had room to stretch ourselves and also take advantage of the pilot's invitation to spend a few minutes up front watching how the whole thing was done.

In the two hour wait at Barbados Airport for our onward connection to Antigua we were fed with rum punches galore, as we were on arrival in every island. They were strong too. We were not to discover until some time later that these rum punches generally included a large measure of the local 'hard' stuff. In St Vincent a friendly waiter demonstrated just what he meant by the local 'hard' stuff when he poured a little on to the counter and set fire to it. Immediately the rum burst into flame. This was what we were being fed on our welcoming ceremony!

Roland became really excited when we took off from Barbados for Antigua. It was dusk. The lights of the island were just beginning to show through although we could still make out the shape of the buildings below as we started to climb away from the airport. Roland had a window seat. He was peering anxiously through the glass when he suddenly shouted 'Look everybody. See that lighthouse down there. See that building not far away. That's were I was brought up. That's where my grandmother lives now.' It was quite a touching scene.

As far as the actual practice facilities were concerned in Antigua, they were not the greatest. The main recreational ground where they were staging a test match for the first time — the fourth of the series — was still being hastily modernised complete with a new double decker stand to be named after Viv Richards. Our training ground owned by the police, was some two or three miles further out from the capital St John's. They were in the process of building a new pavilion, the outfield was rough, the wicket slow and low but it gave us a hint of what was to come.

We arrived in Antigua late on the Thursday evening so the Friday was devoted to a few loosening up exercises to get the stiffness out of our limbs and adjust to the heat. Saturday and Sunday saw us have two long, hard morning net sessions with Monday being devoted to a full scale practice match with running between the wickets and fielding involved.

Some of the players found it exhausting under the hot sun. Personally I enjoyed every minute of it. I am not a sun lover to the extent that I can lie on the beach all day and get bronzed but I can cope with it. I shared a room on that visit with Graham Dilley who is known to us all as 'Picca' for obvious reasons. After taking it easy for five months, slowly building up his strength following his attack of glandular fever towards the end of our season at home, he was ready to prove himself. He worked long and hard in the nets. So long that he was completely exhausted by the time the evening came around. On the second night there he ordered his meal, soup to start with followed by a steak. After his first course he went to his room and that was the last we saw of him. He had put his feet up for just a couple of minutes and went straight off into a deep sleep. Chris Old had double steak that night.

Those early practice sessions were hard. Ken Barrington, assistant manager in charge of cricket, saw to that. But that left the afternoons free to enjoy the tourist attractions. We could not have asked to stay at a better place. Our 'village' was right on the beach with an open air restaurant, the sea no more than twenty yards away. Our apartments were changing hands at anything up to £70,000 a time. Only one hundred yards away along the beach were all manner of water craft. I tried out a sea jet — similar to a motor scooter only adapted for the sea — with Mike Gatting. Others had a go too.

Graham Gooch and John Emburey went sailing. Ian Botham and Bob Willis took themselves off in a pedal boat. Most of us took a trip out to the coral reef three or four miles off shore in a glass bottomed boat. Geoff Boycott? He went off in search of extra nets.

Perhaps the hardest thing to adjust to was the pace of life in the Caribbean. Which was no pace to it at all. Everybody was so friendly. Every request was greeted with the words 'no problem'. Most obviously they were, because it was only on rare occasions that requests were swiftly answered.

It was best summed up by the experience of golfers Brian Huggett and Brian Hutchinson. They were playing in a 'Pro-Am' tournament in Antigua and turned up at the police recreation ground one morning to watch us practice. While they were standing around one stray workman began picking up a few bricks and carrying them to the pavilion which was no more than a shell. He appeared to be the only one working and Brian Hutchinson asked him 'Will you have it finished by Sunday?' 'Oh yes, man,' replied the workman with a smile. 'It will be finished on Sunday. Not this Sunday, not next Sunday but some Sunday.'

I occupied one of the free afternoons by going to see Viv Richards' parents. They live in a modest home almost in the centre of St John's, not far from the prison which is next door to the main ground where Viv made his name whilst still at school and where his father, Malcolm, was a former superintendent. Viv still stays with them whenever he is home although he has had his own flat built adjoining his parents' home to allow them some privacy from his many callers.

They were fine people and obviously proud of what their son has achieved. His father used to be a fast bowler for Antigua and the Leeward Islands in the days when the West Indies Cricket Board of Control refused to look beyond the main centres of Barbados, Jamaica, Trinidad and Guyana for their players. The front room of their house is dominated by the trophies Viv has won all around the world plus action pictures of him on the wall and various team photographs of both the West Indies and Somerset. His younger brother Mervyn is an exact replica. From twenty yards away you could not tell the difference. The same wide shoulders, slim hips, the walk of an old Western gun slinger entering a saloon for the final showdown. Apparently he was rated as good as Viv as a schoolboy cricketer but soccer caught his imagination and he is now the island's top football coach.

In all I suppose those five days, with the setting in which we were living, were as close to paradise as you could expect. Most of the team bought T-shirts saying so. Yet, at the end of it, most of us had had enough. The four days of practice had whetted our appetite for the real thing and we were all eager to get on with the main purpose of the tour which was to play cricket.

The switch from Antigua to Trinidad — with more rum punches waiting for us on arrival — brought problems in that rain made the practice nets at the Queen's Park Oval unusable. They have half a dozen there, three under cover including two concrete pitches and three outdoors including one concrete wicket. None of them was suitable but we were able to get all the practice we needed at the Fatima College ground where the wicket was still slow but the outfield smooth enough to give us a good indication of what it was like in the Caribbean.

Throughout the five days in Antigua and the first two in Trinidad the tour management had stressed that they had not arrived in the West Indies with any preconceived ideas as to the first Test side. With the obvious exception of skipper Ian Botham, the other fifteen members of the party would all stand an equal chance. There is a school of thought — which has a large degree of merit — that this is wrong. That view is that the make up of that first Test side should have been formed before the tour started and given the first chance of getting in practice particularly when we were playing only two four days matches before the first one day international in St Vincent.

That does make sense. As things turned out on this tour, it might have been the better policy with tropical storms washing out the four day match against the Windward Islands and reducing it to two one day games. At the same time the morale of the party as a whole has to be considered. Team spirit plays such an important part on overseas trips when players are away from their homes and families for more than three months at a time. No player must be given the impression from the start that he is among the also rans — his chance of playing in a Test match depending largely on injury to a first choice player rather than form.

But even with that assurance to comfort us, I must say that I was glad I was chosen for the first game even if it did not turn out for the best, at least in my case. The earlier you have a chance of staking a claim the better. I was named to open the innings with Geoff Boycott followed by David Gower at number three, Mike Gatting, Roland Butcher and Both — happily recovered from a ham-string niggle received in Antigua — as the main batsmen. David Bairstow was the wicket-keeper with Peter Willey chosen as the off spinning all rounder and the side completed by Graham Stevenson, Chris Old and Graham Dilley. Geoff Miller, Bob Willis, John Emburey, Paul Downton and Graham Gooch were to share the twelth man duties between them, the four spare men to stay behind in Trinidad for net practice.

It didn't turn out that way. By good fortune 'Dusty' Miller was allotted the twelth man duties that first day of the game against the President's Young West Indies XI and suddenly found himself playing — much to his own surprise because he was forced to send a car back to the hotel in Port of Spain for the rest of his gear. Rain, cricket's oldest enemy, was the cause of the late switch although the weather for the first day of the match could not have been better as we piled into the mini-coach, threaded our way through the Port of Spain rush hour traffic, found the highway through to the San Fernando area and sped along through the acres of sugar cane fields until we hit the immaculate grounds of the Texaco oil refinery.

They owned the sports ground on which we were playing. It was not until a couple of months before the tour was about to start that they were suddenly asked to host the match — with the whole of the playing area having been dug up and relaid with a new drainage system. The outfield was still very rough, the whole area rather short of grass and the new covers purchased for the occasion found to be porous, letting in the rain of the day before on one end of the wicket. That was the reason for the change in team planning. An off spinner working his art on a drying wicket would have been dangerous and 'Dusty' was called in to replace Stevo in case

England fielded first. As it happened Both lost his first toss of the tour and we found ourselves batting.

I did not have a chance of looking at the wicket before we batted. I went out with my bat for a little knock-up, found myself answering to the whistle of physiotherapist Bernard Thomas for our collective limbering up exercises and then had to dash to get ready for the pre-match presentation ceremony. The first opportunity I had to look at the wicket was when I walked out with Geoff to face the new ball.

Most of the opposition were complete strangers to us. We knew Malcolm Marshall from Barbados and Hampshire. He had only recently returned to the West Indies after being one of their star bowlers on the West Indies tour of Pakistan where they had won the four match Test series. Hartley Alleyne, another Barbadian who plays for Worcestershire, was sharing the new ball attack. Their side was being led by Timur Mohamed from Guyana who has proved a prolific run scorer for Suffolk in the Minor Counties for some time and also contained opening batsman cum off spinner Richard Austin who had played Test cricket. The rest were an unknown quantity.

I never had a chance to introduce myself to the rest of the opposition on that first day. I took first strike at the wet end and the first ball from Malcolm was short, ballooned over my head and bounced once more before it reached wicket-keeper Shirlon Williams. It made me wonder a little about what was coming next. I soon discovered.

The next ball was slightly more full in length, got up steeply and I found myself playing it partly off my glove from under my chin. It dropped down harmlessly enough but the reaction was sufficient for Timur to call up an extra short leg. Then came the third delivery, out went the hands of silly mid-on and I was on my way back with a duck against my name and England nought for one. David Gower didn't have to wait long with his pads on. For the next hour while the wicket dried, the going was tough for Geoff and David. It might have been tougher still if the opposition had possessed a third fast bowler to support Marshall and Alleyne but Timur was left with just three spinners to play with once the opening pair finished their stint.

David Gower has been accused of playing too loosely in moments of crisis and getting himself out rather than getting his head down. It was largely the reason why he lost his Test place at home during the summer of 1980 against the West Indies. But nobody could fault his application and determination that morning. I was left on the outside and could only sit and admire the way both he and Geoff tackled the problem, waited for the shine to disappear, the wicket to dry and then enjoy themselves against the rather inexperienced Young West Indies spin attack while they put on 198 runs for the second wicket.

It is true that they both gave chances early on in their innings. Geoff was 36 when he offered a very sharp chance to backward short leg against the off spin of Austin. David gave one chance at 16 driving against Alleyne, another when he was 53 driving against Austin. In all he gave four or five — excited local spectators made it six or seven but some were impossible — during his 187 but considering his four month lay-off after the end of the season at home and the tiring conditions, his innings was still a great booster for the side. If this was the type of Gower the selectors had been searching for over the previous two years, they found him among the storage tanks of Pointe-a-Pierre that day.

The wicket took just over half an hour to dry out completely and from that moment it played easily enough; slow as we all expected with a degree of turn to encourage their spinners. Roger Harper, a seventeen year old schoolboy from Guyana, was the most successful, taking the next five England wickets to fall although they cost him 142 runs off his 43 overs before Both declared at 483 for 6 mid way through the second day.

Harper is a very tall lad, standing over 6ft 2in and one of the most promising youngsters in the Caribbean who is being tipped for future Test honours. He has a touch of Lance Gibbs about him, the way he bowls from right over the top of his head although I felt he might have done better if he had flighted the ball a little more. Against us he was a little too flat and pushed the ball through a little too quickly. The same applied to the other off spinner Austin.

I found the most interesting to be Alston Daniel, a youngster from Tobago who had just forced his way into the Trinidad side. He was a left arm wrist spinner and you don't see many of them around these days. The only other player I've met who bowled 'chinamen' was Bernard Julian, the former Kent and Trinidad all rounder but it was not often that he turned to spin, bowling fast was his first choice. He is still young enough to be playing for Trinidad these days but he is content to live without the game just outside Port of Spain and turned down the invitation to have a trial with Trinidad before they started their Shell Shield competition.

But it was Harper's day, Daniel rolling the ball out of the back of his left hand rather than giving it a tweak which gave our batsmen time to play him off the slow wicket. It was Harper who eventually broke the second wicket partnership when he made one bounce a little more than Boycott expected and the ball rolled off the underside of Boycott's right arm on to his wicket. He had made 87 and Harper bowled him for exactly the same score in the second innings to give him a match he'll remember for some time. He became quite a celebrity having bowled Boycott twice and looked most embarrassed when a waitress shyly thrust a dollar note in front of him and asked him for his autograph. It's probably the first time he had been asked.

With Boycott's dismissal Mike Gatting went in to play probably the most entertaining innings of the day. It took him only sixty-seven minutes to reach his first 50 against a tiring attack and everything he hit seemed to come off the middle of the bat. Following the shock of my early dismissal, the tough hour that followed against Marshall and Alleyne on a drying wicket, we had done well to recover to 330 for two at the close, Gower having reached the first century of the tour some time before the end of play.

He went on to score 187 with nineteen fours and two sixes before he was caught at slip attempting to cut. Mike Gatting missed a deserved century by six runs when he was bowled attempting to run the ball down to third man and Roland Butcher and Both chased runs quickly before our declaration came.

Two of their batsmen impressed me immediately during their innings of 320. Both are from Jamaica, which has not been providing many batsmen to the West Indies team in recent years, the unfortunate Lawrence Rowe apart. I'm sure that Everton Mattis and Jeffrey Dujon will rectify that situation in the years ahead.

Mattis, a tall twenty-three year old with a very straight forward approach who drives the ball superbly, was the first to benefit from his performances against us when he scored 41 and 46. He was later chosen for the first one day international in St Vincent in the absence of Viv Richards who was bothered by sinus trouble and made their Test team.

Yet I thought that Dujon, a twenty-two year old, looked slightly the better player against us and it did not surprise me to read a fortnight later that he had scored another century for Jamaica against Barbados in a Shell Shield match when Jamaica had lost their first five wickets for less than 100. Admittedly we helped him to his unbeaten 105 against us by giving him a couple of lives in our first full day in the field but he still showed himself to be a fine wristy player who produced some impressive strokes through the leg side. Mattis was far more casual, a batsman who would be in trouble in English conditions until he adapted his style to counter the ball moving away from him.

We also learned some valuable lessons. We learnt that it was essential for the faster bowlers to bowl a steady line and length the whole time in Caribbean conditions, almost waiting for the batsmen to make a mistake, the odd ball to do something off the wicket and not to be able to bowl people out with deliveries that take wickets in England. Dilley had a frustrating opening spell finding very little bounce or movement and was punished for it but had learned the lesson by the time he returned. We also discovered that it was better to field a yard or so deeper than we would in England to give us more time to judge the speed of the ball through the thinner air. It comes at you faster than you expect.

Considering it was our first experience in the field we were all reasonably happy at earning a 163 run first innings lead with a chance of having a longish knock in the second innings before Both had to make his token declaration. I was happy with the way things went in the second innings, and grateful to Geoff. Many people find him difficult to get along with and he would be the first to admit he is very much his own man yet he is sensitive to the feelings of others particularly in cricket. I went out the second time expecting to face the first ball again but Geoff offered to take first strike remembering my duck. There is always that extra tension around the first ball of the match and it was a great help in my situation — facing a pair — seeing Geoff face up to it instead.

I was more than satisfied with my 43 because of the way Marshall bowled. He had been handicapped by a slight hamstring strain in the first innings. I don't think he was too happy to be playing in the match either, having to prove himself again after just returning from the West Indies tour of Pakistan. Bowling in the second innings he was conscious that he was being watched by two of the three West Indies selectors. Steve Camacho, the former Guyana and West Indies opening batsman was managing the Young West Indies side and Clyde Walcott had flown in to join him.

Malcolm knew he was being closely watched. He was also helped by the fact that the weather became cloudy on the third afternoon and he explained to me afterwards that cloud always helps him obtain movement off the wicket in the Caribbean. That third afternoon he was certainly a shade faster than he had been at any time in the Test series in England eight months before. He worried us all and again when he bowled on the fourth morning.

He bowled one to me which pitched middle and leg and went over the off stump. He bowled another later which pitched off stump and went over middle and leg but I managed to survive. Batting for some time with Geoff in our 114 run opening partnership I also appreciated what a magnificent player he is of spin bowling. He has often said he wished he had been playing cricket in the thirties when there was more spin bowling around than you find today and I can see why. He would have scored thousands more than he has today.

I was seven short of my half century when Marshall accounted for me, a thick inside edge on to my thigh and then on to the wicket. David Bairstow, promoted in the order to give him some batting practice, fell just four deliveries later. When Geoff was again denied his century on the last morning by Harper, it was just a question of getting runs quickly for Both and Roland again before the declaration at lunchtime. It was not made with any real hope of producing a result, more a gesture to the crowd and to give our bowlers another chance of practice. Peter Willey and Geoff Miller took that chance well.

The target of 372 to win in four hours was never on but the early Young West Indies batsmen never seemed to appreciate that. Openers Richard Austin and Richard Gabriel and even skipper Timor went gaily after the runs. They perished. 'Dusty' Miller dismissed both openers, beating them through the air while Timor, who had hit eight fours in his 35, was bowled by Peter Willey off his pads. Three wickets had gone down for 93 runs and Both started putting on the pressure.

As the younger batsmen came in we could see clearly that they were nervous, and must not be given time to settle. We always felt that when one wicket fell, we could get another straight away and so it proved. We were held up once immediately after a small shower and the tea interval when Marshall joined Mattis but when Mattis was bowled by Dusty just after the start of the last twenty overs attempting a wild looking drive, the rest was comparatively easy. Apart from the tea interval, Dusty bowled his 26.2 overs without a break and enjoyed himself immensely finishing with six for 70. That gave him 9 for 139 in a match he was not down to play.

I feel there was one particular lesson to be learned from the match. Care should be taken on the next tour here to avoid if possible the players having to endure cramped, hour long coach journeys before and after play. The dressing room facilities at Guaracara Park were not the best. We were forced to sit in the mini-coach in all our sticky gear and once back at our hotel in Port of Spain found the hot water system had broken down. We were left sore and very stiff which did not help.

In 1968 when England played a two day match on the same ground the players stayed privately with officials of the Texaco oil company. They enjoyed having the players and wanted to do the same thing this time. They went out of their way to look after us and it would have been preferable to that coach journey.

Despite that first innings duck, I was reasonably satisfied with what I had achieved. I was delighted when I was also picked for the second four day match against the Windward Islands in St Vincent. Unfortunately tropical storms struck to wash out the first two days and two one day matches were arranged instead.

The tour selectors juggled with the side but I still remained to open the innings with Graham Gooch in the first match. It might have been better if I had not. I made only one before I was caught behind off Winston Davis in the third over of the match. There was nothing I could do about it. It was one of the best deliveries I'd faced for some time, moving away late when I was already into my stroke and just caught the edge. People who were sitting behind the bowler's arm later told me it was the best delivery in the match. That was nice to know but it didn't really help my mood.

PRESIDENT'S YOUNG WEST INDIES XI *v.* ENGLAND
TRINIDAD, JANUARY 23–26

England

	First Innings		*Second Innings*	
B. C. Rose	c Payne b Marshall	0	b Marshall	43
G. Boycott	b Harper	87	b Harper	87
D. I. Gower	c Mattis b Harper	187		
M. W. Gatting	b Harper	94		
R. O. Butcher	c and b Harper	42	not out	20
*I. T. Botham	b Harper	11	c Payne b Alleyne	33
P. Willey	not out	16	c Williams b Marshall	10
G. Miller	not out	12	not out	4
+D. L. Bairstow	(did not bat)		lbw b Marshall	0
Extras	b7, lb 7, w 2, nb 18	34	lb 5, w 3, nb 3	11
Total	(six wickets dec.)	483	(five wickets dec.)	208

Fall of wickets: 1—0, 2—198, 3—396, 4—404, 5—446, 6—457.
1—114, 2—114, 3—134, 4—179, 5—187.
C. M. Old and G. R. Dilley did not bat

Bowling: First Innings — Marshall 25—9—54—1; Alleyne 27—5—62—0; Harper 43—6—142—5; Daniel 21—6—58—0; Austin 39—8—133—0.
Second Innings — Marshall 18—4—48—3; Alleyne 19—1—46—1; Daniel 16—5—36—0; Harper 23—5—58—1; Austin 6—2—9—0.

West Indies

	First Innings		Second Innings	
R. Austin	c Miller b Botham	25	b Miller	19
R. Gabriel	run out	22	c Bairstow b Miller	22
*Timur Mohamed	b Miller	37	b Willey	35
E. Mattis	c Miller b Dilley	41	b Miller	46
T. Payne	st Bairstow b Miller	1	b Miller	1
H. Alleyne	b Willey	33	lbw b Miller	6
J. Dujon	not out	105	c Botham b Willey	1
+S. Williams	c Old b Miller	13	c Gatting b Willey	4
M. Marshall	c Old b Botham	27	run out	31
R. Harper	lbw b Botham	0	lbw b Miller	0
A. Daniel	c Gower b Old	0	not out	0
Extras	b 7, lb 4, nb 5	16	b 8, lb 4, nb 4	16
Total		320		181

Fall of wickets: 1—38, 2—68, 3—123, 4—127, 5—133, 6—193, 7—230, 8—319, 9—319.
1—37, 2—56, 3—93, 4—94, 5—95, 6—159, 7—170, 8—171, 9—175.

Bowling: First innings — Dilley 22—1—104—1; Old 13.3—4—34—1; Botham 12—0—43—3; Miller 26—8—69—3; Willey 16—3—54—1; Second innings — Dilley 10—3—18—0; Botham 4—0—21—0; Miller 26.2—9—70—6; Old 4—0—27—0; Willey 17—6—29—3.

* captain + wicket-keeper

England won by 190 runs

3 GRAHAM STEVENSON (YORKSHIRE & ENGLAND)

Windward Islands *v.* England (One Day Match)

1–2 February

One Day International

4 February

Delight of Graham Stevenson at being included in the tour party and decription of St Vincent. Four day match against the Windward Islands changed to two limited-over one day matches because of rain.

It is not Dusty Miller's fault that he was born a few miles the wrong side of the border which stops him being a Yorkshireman. He is almost one of us and he has my complete sympathy that he arrived in this world in Chesterfield and is forced to play for Derbyshire instead. Not everybody is perfect. There was one moment on the tour when I admit I wondered why he had been born at all!

There are always one or two players in any touring party who miss out. Players who find themselves relegated to the role of being a spare man, often through no fault of their own. In most cases it is an accident. Loss of form at the wrong time; perhaps an injury or a simple unlucky break. Twelve months earlier I had found myself something of a spare part on England's tour of Australia. By the time I arrived to join the party as a replacement for the injured Mike Hendrick, the shape of the Test side and the one day international side for the Benson and Hedges World Series Cup had already been shaped.

Along with Wayne Larkins of Northants who had missed out on one of the early batting roles, I became one of the 'fill in' men. We played in the other matches when the Test players took a well deserved break, played in perhaps one match a fortnight. It took both Wayne and myself a couple of months to prove ourselves in this way, we forced our way into the one day side and, in my case, I clinched my first Test cap in the Golden Jubilee Test against India in Bombay on our way home. I was one of the proudest men on earth that day when Mike Brearley, our captain on the 1979—80 tour of Australia and India, called me aside and told me I was in. The England cap I had dreamt about for so long was finally on my head. Not that I had much of an opportunity to show anybody what I might have been capable of with Ian Botham scoring a century, taking wickets in both Indian innings and the match over well inside the distance with England winning by ten wickets.

I couldn't have been more pleased either when I was called aside on this tour and told that I would be playing in the opening match against the Young West Indies XI at Pointe-a-Pierre in Trinidad. If I was going to be a spare man on this tour it would partly be my own fault. Right from the start this time I was going to be given my chance to show what I would do. Until it rained, that is, in the Caribbean dry season and until the brand new covers at Pointe-a-Pierre let water on to the wicket, when Ian Botham, manager Alan Smith and assistant manager Ken Barrington had a look at the strip and decided the conditions were ready made for a spinner. That let me out and let Dusty in. It was only by chance that Dusty was there, having drawn the short straw that morning for twelth man duties. I could have cursed him. I think I did!

Don't get me wrong. There is nothing lowering about being a spare man on a touring party. Every member of the sixteen strong side is essential for the overall success of the tour. Those who are not actually playing still have a vital role to play. But it can be very frustrating sitting on the sidelines, perhaps getting a knock or a bowl once a fortnight when all you want to do is play cricket the whole time.

I was very grateful for the fact that I was in the West Indies at all. After my Test debut in Bombay I hadn't really got near the England side at home against the West Indies the following summer or for the Centenary Test against Australia at Lord's. I was told by Both or one of the selectors during the summer that I was still under consideration but the nearest I got to actually playing was in the final Test against the West Indies at Headingley when I was named in the England twelve only to be left out on the final morning.

As far as a place in the tour party was concerned, I faced considerable competition from Surrey's Robin Jackman who had a magnificent summer at home, taking more than one hundred wickets for the first time. When he was picked for the one day international against Australia and then named in the squad for the Centenary Test, I thought he would be a certainty to go on tour and I would be spending winter at home.

I must confess the wheel of the car wobbled a little when I heard my name among the touring party when it was announced a week after the season had finished. Strangely enough I was driving down to London with my wife Angela heading for the West Indies — Antigua to be precise — on a cricketing/holiday mission playing for Leicestershire's Barry Dudleston in a benefit exercise. I wanted to hear my name called out and was still surprised when I heard it.

As it turned out, it was probably better that I missed that first game. It meant that I was assured of a place in the side for the second match, scheduled to be a four day affair against the Windward Islands in St Vincent. It undoubtedly suited me that the first two days were washed out by unseasonal tropical storms which played their own calypso tunes on the corrugated roofed huts and homes which dotted the hillside — some pitched precariously on steep slopes — overlooking the capital of Kingstown, a really old fashioned Caribbean centre unspoilt by tourism. Instead of the four day match two one day matches of 50 overs each side were arranged. I couldn't afford to bowl anything loose in those especially with the first one day international over the same course to follow in St Vincent one day later.

I was ready to play cricket by the time the first one day match came along. St Vincent is a beautiful island at the head of a series of islands known as the Grenadines. On a clear day — there were not too many while we were there — you could see Mustique where Princess Margaret holidays in the Caribbean. I can understand why she goes there to get away from it all. Nine of us went over in a private plane for a look around but there was hardly anything to see. Perhaps one hotel, small at that, miles of beaches and little else. Once there, you really feel completely cut off from the rest of the world. A real Robinson Crusoe island with nothing to do but relax in the sun when it shines.

There is quite a bit to see in St Vincent itself. It has a population of just over 100,000 and many work on the land in the banana plantations, tobacco fields, coconut plantations etc. The government has refused to allow the tourist trade to take over the island and insists that the land is cultivated. There are small holdings on every hillside no matter how steep. The island has an active volcano called Mount Soufrière which had erupted two years earlier, spilling its contents over the land and ruining the banana crop. Eight months before we arrived the banana crop had been ruined again by Hurricane Allen which damaged homes and schools.

The inhabitants of St Vincent had gone through a rough time in the previous two years before our visit. We went through a rough two days after landing because of the tropical storms which swept over the mountains and cascaded down in a seemingly never ending stream. The rain ruined what practice facilities the local groundsman had attempted to get ready for us. When the sun is shining and the sea and beach beckons, the Caribbean can be a marvellous place. When it rains, time drags. There is just nothing to do but sit in the hotel and stare forlornly out of the window. There are no other attractions on such occasions.

That is why I felt ready to play when the rain eventually gave over. I had been in the Caribbean almost a fortnight by then without turning my arm over in a proper competition. The actual ground itself is quaint, sandwiched between the Caribbean sea behind the sightscreen at one end and the island's only airstrip at the other. I was told that before they erected a couple of small stands to 'hide' the runway, cricket used to be brought to a halt everytime a plane took off or landed right behind the bowler's arm. They used to stop the traffic too, because the main road around the island went straight across the middle of the runway.

When we actually got down to playing the two one day matches against the Windward Islands, the opposition wasn't really as strong as we would have liked although they were enough for us to cope with considering our lack of practice. They played under a handicap in that their side had been chosen for a four day game. They had included three spin bowlers, including a leg spinner and their attack was not best suited to the demands of a limited over match.

Despite that we didn't make the progress we expected after Both had won the toss and decided to bat first. The wicket didn't help. It was so slow that stroke making was difficult. The ball never came on to the bat. The wicket itself was not completely trustworthy and a few doubts were put in our head when we saw Brian Rose get out to one which moved very late off the wicket and found the edge.

We were always struggling to make any significant progress after that. Even Graham Gooch, who never wastes an opportunity to score, took an hour getting into double figures before offering a return catch against one of the two off spinners Thomas Kentish. Both and Roland Butcher briefly entertained the small crowd with a six each in their innings. I briefly entertained them by getting a nick against the first ball I received to give a catch behind and it was left to Paul Downton to carry us to a reasonable 166 for nine at the end of our 40 overs.

Our victory margin was 16 runs in the end, which sounds close but the Windward Island batsmen never really threatened to beat us. Their batting wasn't up to it apart from that of their captain Irving Shillingford who played four Tests for the West Indies in the middle 1970s. He and leg spinner Monty Warner held us up for a while when adding 45 for the third wicket until Shillingford provided me with my first wicket of the tour. He attempted to pull me through mid wicket but misjudged his stroke and David Gower obliged with the catch at deepish square leg. That was my only wicket of the innings but I was satisfied with my eight overs which cost only 22 runs. Normally it takes me three or four matches when I start a season at home to find my length, line and rhythm but everything slipped into place right from the first ball in St Vincent.

The Windward Islands were still 16 runs short when they had used up their overs but we had suffered one setback. Having his first bowl of the tour Bob Willis, our vice captain, twisted his left knee when his foot slipped into a rut in the run-up at one end. He was forced to limp off and the injury was serious enough to put him out of the first Test.

The Windward Islands batsmen extended us a little more in the second game the following day before we got home by six wickets with thirteen deliveries to spare. This match should have been 50 overs each side like the first but we ended up with a different set of rules. The first match had been kept down to 40 overs each side because a damp outfield had delayed the start. The second match was suddenly extended to 55 overs each side half way through the Windward Island innings when the umpires and the scoreboard operator got themselves involved in a mix-up.

Each bowler should have been limited to 10 overs. According to the scoreboard Peter Willey had bowled only nine overs of his off spin when Both turned to him again. He had bowled five deliveries of his new over when a complete stranger — who later turned out to be one of the broadcasters from a local radio station — came running on to the field and informed the umpires that Willey was, in fact, bowling his eleventh over. After a mid-field conference, a quick check with the official scorers and no doubt a telling off for the scoreboard operator, the umpires decided to extend the match to 55 overs to get themselves out of their predicament.

A left handed batsman by the name of Lancelot John who has played for the Combined Islands in the Shell Shield made the best of the situation for the Windward Islands. He opened the innings and stayed through 36 overs until he was trapped leg before by Graham Gooch who turned out to be our most successful bowler by taking 3 for 23 with his off cutters. Irving Shillingford again made a useful contribution with his 31 runs but the rest generally struggled as all six of us who bowled concentrated on getting our line and length right in our final practice before the one day international.

I had to wait until the last batsman before I managed to get a wicket when a delivery kept low and took the off stump. Again I was reasonably satisfied with how I had performed, my nine point two overs costing just 25 runs even though I didn't manage to bowl a maiden. Nobody had managed to get after me.

The Windward Islands were all out for 183 and that left us an asking rate of less than three and a half runs an over. Not too demanding in the circumstances. With the match being played over 55 overs, it also presented our batsmen a chance of playing a proper innings which Graham Gooch certainly needed having had only one previous visit to the middle. He didn't waste the opportunity. He had a very good and hard look at the bowling before taking any chances. It was not until the tenth over of the innings that he hit England's first four. With Geoff Boycott equally watchful as ever at the other end, the pair put down the foundation of our victory platform by seeing 89 on the scoreboard before Gooch mistimed a drive to extra cover after he had scored exactly 50.

From that moment things started to go a little adrift. Brian Rose had made only three when he played on attempting to pull the left arm opening bowler Joseph Jack. David Gower had made only six when he was brilliantly stumped by a lively wicket-keeper who goes by the name of Ignatious Cadette and Peter Willey was caught low at cover after he had made 11. There were five and a half overs left at that stage with another 33 runs wanted for victory. The asking rate had gone up and that was when Both decided to put 'Plan B' into operation. That's me. I was promoted four places up the order but it wasn't exactly an emergency situation with Both himself, Roland Butcher and David Bairstow still to come. 'Don't worry skipper,' I told him as I went out to Geoff Boycott. 'You just leave it to us Yorkies.'

Not that I was feeling particularly confident after my first ball duck the previous day. Dusty Miller insisted I was going to get another one and I waved the bat in triumph at him when the first ball I received went down the leg side and I managed to get a nick on it to get off the mark. I managed to slog 19 including one stroke for three through mid wicket which surprised a lot of people who believe I hit everything through extra cover. Boics managed to slog a few as well towards the end of his unbeaten 85 and we were there with thirteen deliveries to spare. Three matches, three victories and even if the opposition was not the highest standard you can't ask for a better record than that to enter the first one day international.

It had to rain again first, of course, which ruined our final net practice on the spare day in between the games. Poor Graham Dilley was sent to work his aggression off against the sight screen when he dropped one short just after the net session started and it reared over Both's head. That put an end to that net session. The four Yorkshire players plus Peter Willey went off in search of a concrete wicket Geoff Boycott had heard about on the other side of the runway and we managed to get in a session on that. After we had cleared it of the goats, pigs, sheep and various other animals using the field and the small boys who later proved useful in fetching the ball. At least the batsmen had some decent practice although the run-ups were so rough I couldn't turn my arm over properly.

I heard that afternoon that I was in England's twelve for the one day international and I thought I stood a chance of making the side after the way I had bowled in the two one day games against the Windward Islands. Obviously Geoff Boycott and Graham Gooch would open the innings. Peter Willey was named as number three after Rose's unfortunate start to the tour. David Gower, Roland Butcher, Both and Mike Gatting were to fill the next four batting positions with David Bairstow the wicket-keeper. John Emburey, Graham Dilley, Chris Old and myself filled the squad, one of us to drop out on the final morning. Dill made any decision making unnecessary when he reported a stomach upset on the morning of the match.

We had already heard two day's before that Viv Richards would be missing from the West Indies side because of sinus trouble which was a great boost to our hopes. Gordon Greenidge was also missing which was a help as well. He has had a habit of hitting us hard in recent years. He had not been considered because he had not been fit to play for Barbados at that point after returning home early from the West Indies tour of Pakistan late in 1980 because of spinal trouble. They were also lacking Sylvester Clarke of Barbados and Surrey who had received a fifteen day ban following a brick throwing incident in West Indies' final Test in Pakistan during which a spectator had been hit on the head.

That still left them with a formidable team as Both was to

remind us with Desmond Haynes and Faoud Bacchus to open the innings followed by newcomer Everton Mattis, Alvin Kallicharran and Clive Lloyd — who had both hit big centuries for Guyana against Trinidad the week before — and Larry Gomes. David Murray was the wicket-keeper with Andy Roberts, Joel Garner, Mike Holding and Colin Croft completing the side. Powerful indeed but one we felt we could handle particularly on a slowish wicket.

The whole island had been looking forward to their first representative match for months. Few people had watched the two games against the Windward Islands but it seemed everybody was there on the morning of the international, many clambering over the walls to get in for nothing, the stands packed to bursting point, people hanging on to every vantage point. On the morning of the match a small freighter anchored in the bay right behind one sightscreen and a couple of crew clambered up the mast and sat perched up there all day with a perfect view right behind the bowler's arm.

The day itself was bright when Both won the toss and put the West Indies in. Although we started the match in a confident mood everything went better than we expected when we bowled them out for 127 in 47.2 overs. There was the odd minor mishap in the field but nothing costly in a performance which surprised me considering our shortage of practice. Only Haynes and Mattis on the West Indies side managed to reach double figures as we were given an object lesson on how to bowl by Chris Old right from the start. His first five overs cost just eight runs and those eight were two fours by Haynes made more in desperation than anything else trying to break the hold Chilly had over the batsmen. Apart from one loose over which cost 15 runs, Both was almost as mean when he shared the new ball and helped to strengthen our belief that the West Indies batsmen soon lose patience when they are made to struggle for runs.

Faoud Bacchus, for instance, had struggled painfully against Chilly trying to get the ball away when he lost patience and pulled desperately at one outside the off stump which went straight into my hands at deepish mid-on. The West Indies are five for one in the fifth over and the slide was on.

In an attempt to break loose, Haynes threw his bat at everything that was slightly off line and had scored 32 of his 34 runs in boundaries when he became my first victim in my second over. I had taken over from Chilly and I had the impression when I let the ball go that Haynes was going to try to smash me to the boundary whatever I bowled. He stepped out of his crease, swung across the line and John Emburey took a fine catch, high to his right, at square leg to leave the West Indies on 48 for 2 in the thirteenth over.

Emburey had taken over from Both at the other end and captured the next wicket when Kallicharran was beaten through the air as he attempted to drive and three overs later Clive Lloyd became my second victim although I couldn't have given him out from where I stood. He stepped back in that lazy manner of his and attempted to drive me square of the wicket but Peter Willey took the catch low down by his left ankle at deepish backward point. From where I stood I wasn't sure it was a catch until I saw Pete's reaction. Clive stood a second until Pete indicated it was clean. He told me when I went to congratulate him that he knew it was clean by the way the ball had knocked the back of his hands into the ground which could only have happened if the ball had been dropping downwards and not going up again after it had bounced.

From that moment it became a procession. Peter Willey, making the odd ball turn viciously, claimed the next wicket, the thoroughly deserved one of Larry Gomes after he had completely beaten him half a dozen times in the three or four previous overs. Graham Gooch came on to claim the next two having David Murray bowled and seeing Andy Roberts brilliantly stumped by David Bairstow. The collapse gathered momentum as the tail came and went, two of the last three wickets falling to run-outs including the West Indies batting hero Everton Mattis.

It must have been a bewildering experience for him in his first senior representative game, the newcomer watching his far more experienced colleagues coming and going in quick succession. Not until he made himself the victim of the last run-out to close the innings did he panic. Until then he had batted with complete authority, picking up runs where he could during his 43 over stay, hardly playing a false stroke. Without him, they would have been in a complete mess. We shall be seeing a lot of him in the future.

Both surprised many people towards the end of the West Indies innings by not calling upon Chilly again to finish his last five overs after the way he had bowled his first five. Both used himself instead — with me at the other end — although he had been our most costly bowler. The reason is fairly simple. Because of his accuracy and length Chilly is not quite so effective when the slog is on as we have seen once or twice in Yorkshire while Both does bowl a good delivery into the block hole as he showed when taking the wicket of Michael Holding in his second spell.

We should have won the match. Whatever excuses we might be able to put forward to explain how the match got away from us by just two runs, there is no escaping the fact that we did not bat well. We had the match won when we bowled them out for 127. We lost it when we were 15 for 4 half way through the eighth over of our innings. Won it back again when Both and David Gower joined together for a 65 run partnership in 26 overs for the fifth wicket and finally lost it at the death.

It all started to go wrong in the sixth over, the third from Colin Croft when we lost Boycott, caught at second slip following one which left him and Willey who got a thin edge to be taken behind. In the next over from Roberts, Gooch launched himself into a drive only to edge to slip and one over later Roland Butcher was caught behind. Four wickets gone only 15 runs on the board and it might have been even worse if David Murray had accepted a stumping chance when Both was 22. Clive Lloyd had gambled on Kallicharran's off spin rather than Gomes' medium paced cutters for his fifth bowler and we could not even get Kalli away.

Slowly Both and David Gower pulled us round until David drove at Kalli and was caught in the covers from a stroke he will regret. He had done a fine job however and the match looked ours once again, until Lloyd looked in Croft's direction. He had taken three wickets in his first spell and came back to dismiss Mike Gatting and David Bairstow in his second. He returned once more to end Both's resistance in his third spell, having him caught behind. He still had one over left when I walked out to join John Emburey with 14 runs wanted and five overs remaining. It was still our match at that point.

It was then that Clive Lloyd took his big gamble and one which was to work. Although Croft had been their dangerman with figures of 6 for 15 from his nine overs of cutters bowled at a brisk pace on a responsive wicket, Clive waved Croft away when he came up to bowl his last over and turned to the pace of Holding instead. Although Croft had taken the wickets he does not possess the control that Holding does and Clive gambled that Holding would be far more difficult to score against in a tense situation even if he didn't take a wicket. He proved difficult to score against, and he took the wicket.

We needed five runs to win when Holding started the forty-seventh over and bowled Emburey. We needed three runs to win when Holding started the forty-ninth over (and his last) and he bowled Chilly with second ball to set the island of St Vincent dancing with delight. We were all bitterly disappointed after the way we had bowled and fielded. Both must have been close to despair after the way he had dragged us back into the game with his thirty-seven over stay for his 60 following our early collapse. It was a tremendous match for the people of St Vincent, one I'm sure they will not forget in a hurry. Yes, a tremendous game of cricket — with the wrong result.

WINDWARD ISLANDS v. ENGLAND (one day 40 over match)
ST VINCENT, FEBRUARY 1

England

G. A. Gooch	c and b Kentish	13
B. C. Rose	c Cadette b Davis	1
R. O. Butcher	c Hinds b Kentish	44
*I. T. Botham	st Cadette b Hinds	31
D. I. Gower	b Jack	14
M. W. Gatting	c Browne b Hinds	16
G. B. Stevenson	c Cadette b Jack	0
+P. R. Downton	not out	23
J. E. Emburey	c Shillingford b Davis	3
G. R. Dilley	c Sebastien b Hinds	7
R. G. D. Willis	not out	0
Extras	b 5, w 1, nb 8	14
Total	(nine wickets, 40 overs)	166

Fall of wickets: 1—6, 2—43, 3—76, 4—111, 5—116, 6—116, 7—138, 8—152, 9—161

Bowling: Davis 8—0—17—2; Jack 8—1—23—2; Warner 8—1—32—0; Kentish 8—1—21—2; Hinds 8—0—59—3

Windward Islands

L. Sebastien	c Botham b Willis	9
L. John	c Botham b Dilley	17
M. Warner	c Botham b Gooch	24
*I. Shillingford	c Gower b Stevenson	26
C. Browne	lbw b Botham	16
S. Hinds	c sub b Dilley	7
J. Guiste	c Rose b Botham	3
+I. Cadette	not out	17
W. Davis	c Gooch b Dilley	7
T. Kentish	lbw b Botham	0
J. Jack	not out	4
Extras	b 1, lb 8, w I, nb 10	20
Total	(nine wickets, 40 overs)	150

Fall of wickets: 1—31, 2—31, 3—76, 4—107, 5—111, 6—118, 7—118, 8—136, 9—136

Bowling: Willis 7—0—30—1; Dilley 8—0—28—3; Stevenson 8—1—22—1; Botham 8—0—30—3; Emburey 8—1—18—0; Gooch 1—0—2—1

* captain + wicket-keeper

England won by 16 runs

WINDWARD ISLANDS *v*. ENGLAND (55 overs match)
ST VINCENT, FEBRUARY 2

Windward Islands		
L. Sebastien	lbw b Botham	9
L. John	lbw b Gooch	58
*I. Shillingford	c Gooch b Willey	31
M. Warner	c and b Gooch	3
C. Browne	b Old	20
H. Williams	st Bairstow b Gooch	9
+I. Cadette	run out	10
S. Hinds	not out	18
W. Davis	lbw b Old	0
K. Hobson	b Stevenson	4
J. Jack	run out	5
Extras	b 3, lb 8, nb 5	16
Total	(53.2 overs)	183

Fall of wickets: 1—33, 2—90, 3—109, 4—116, 5—129, 6—151, 7—156, 8—157, 9—174.

Bowling: Old 9—0—34—2; Botham 7—1—21—1; Stevenson 9.2—0—25—1; Willey 11—1—23—1; Emburey 11—0—41—0; Gooch 6—1—23—3.

England		
G. Boycott	not out	85
G. A. Gooch	c sub b Warner	50
B. C. Rose	b Jack	3
D. I. Gower	st Cadette b Hobson	6
P. Willey	c sub b Hobson	11
G. B. Stevenson	not out	19
Extras	b 1, lb 2, w 1, nb 6	10
Total	(four wickets, 52.5 overs)	184

R. O. Butcher, *I. T. Botham, + D. L. Bairstow, J. E. Emburey and C. M. Old did not bat.

Fall of wickets: 1—89, 2—118, 3—132, 4—151.

Bowling: Davis 10—3—26—0; Jack 9.5—3—26—1; Hobson 11—1—46—2; Warner 11—0—46—1; Hinds 11—0—30—0.

* captain + wicket-keeper

England won by 6 wickets

WEST INDIES v. ENGLAND (one-day international)
ST VINCENT, FEBRUARY 4

West Indies		
D. L. Haynes	c Emburey b Stevenson	34
S. F. A. Bacchus	c Stevenson b Old	1
E. Mattis	run out	62
A. I. Kallicharran	b Emburey	2
*C. H. Lloyd	c Willey b Stevenson	2
H. A. Gomes	b Willey	8
+D. A. Murray	b Gooch	1
A. M. E. Roberts	st Bairstow b Gooch	2
J. Garner	run out	4
M. A. Holding	b Botham	1
C. E. H. Croft	not out	2
Extras	lb 4, w 1, nb 3	8
Total	(47.2 overs)	127

Fall of wickets: 1—5, 2—48, 3—51, 4—58, 5—89, 6—90, 7—102, 8—110, 9—120

Bowling: Old 5—4—8—1; Botham 8—1—32—1; Stevenson 8.2—2—18—2; Emburey 10—4—20—1; Willey 10—1—29—1; Gooch 6—1—12—2.

England		
G. Boycott	c Mattis b Croft	2
G. A. Gooch	c Lloyd b Roberts	11
P. Willey	c Murray b Croft	0
D. I. Gower	c Haynes b Kallicharran	23
R. O. Butcher	c Murray b Croft	1
*I. T. Botham	c Murray b Croft	60
M. W. Gatting	b Croft	3
+D. L. Bairstow	b Croft	5
J. E. Emburey	b Holding	5
G. B. Stevenson	not out	6
C. M. Old	b Holding	1
Extras	lb 8	8
Total	(48.2 overs)	125

Fall of wickets: 1—14, 2—14, 3—14, 4—15, 5—80, 6—88, 7—111, 8—114, 9—123

Bowling: Roberts 10—1—30—1; Holding 9.2—2—30—2; Croft 9—4—15—6; Garner 10—2—17—0; Kallicharran 10—3—25—1

* captain   + wicket-keeper

West Indies won by 2 runs

4 PETER WILLEY (NORTHANTS & ENGLAND)

Trinidad & Tobago *v.* England

7–10 February

Peter Willey complains of the lack of practice facilities in Trinidad and of the team's lack of practice against high quality fast bowlers. He tells of Trinidad's new bowling discovery, Harold Joseph, and describes the match against Trinidad and Tobago.

Our two run defeat in the one day international in St Vincent had highlighted what we had been lacking on the tour so far — regular practice against high quality fast bowlers. With only the four day match against Trinidad and Tobago to come before the opening Test match of the series, we were all in desperate need of a fairly long exposure against pace to sharpen our reflexes and reactions ready to counter the type of attack we could expect when we met up with Clive Lloyd again. Unfortunately we were not to find it on our return to Port of Spain.

Events had not run in our favour since the opening match of the tour against the Young West Indies XI in Pointe-a-Pierre. Our mood following the one day international defeat wasn't helped when we learned at short notice that we had to be up with the humming bird for a dawn departure from our hotel for the flight back to Trinidad because the times had been changed. We were all so tired by the time we eventually got to Port of Spain, the management had no alternative but to cancel the planned practice session. And the one the following day because the nets at the Queen's Park Oval, home of the Test centre in Port of Spain, had not been made ready in time despite repeated pleas from assistant manager Ken Barrington.

Throughout the tour we had struggled for decent practice facilities and a grave shortage of net bowlers. Normally on tours the host club provide any amount of youngsters willing to have a bowl in the nets at visiting batsmen. On this tour so far they had been conspicuous by their absence. Worse was to follow when the match actually started. There was time for only twenty-one deliveries after former West Indies Test wicket-keeper and Trinidad captain Deryck Murray had won the toss and put us in. Yet another violent storm — constant companions of ours over the previous fortnight — washed out the morning session. It had just started to dry after an hour of sun when another storm washed out play for the day. This, when all of us were feeling particularly rusty. I've had more practice at home to start a season than I had had on the tour so far with the opening Test of the series less than a week away.

I went into the match in desperate need of a long innings in the middle if I was to feel right for the Test. In the first innings in Pointe-a-Pierre I had gone in when the search was on for quick runs with a declaration coming up. In the second innings I had not lasted long before Malcolm Marshall got me. In the second one day match against the Windward Islands quick runs were again the order of the day and in the one day international I had lasted just four deliveries against Colin Croft. I was far from ready as a batsman. As an off spinner too I felt the need of a long spell. Spinners need to bowl a minimum of 15 overs a day for several days a week to keep in their groove. At that stage I had bowled only 54 overs in three weeks largely because of the weather and England's short programme before the real battle commenced.

Going into the Trinidad and Tobago match I felt very much on trial. With our shortage of batting practice I couldn't really see us going into the first Test with three off spinners — Dusty Miller, John Emburey and myself. All three had been picked against Trinidad and I felt the selectors would have a long look to decide which two to take into the Test.

Graham Gooch needed to play his first first class match of the tour. Geoff Boycott needed to get the feel of the Trinidad wicket. Brian Rose was wanted for the number three position and David Gower obviously had to play despite his good form until then. A foot injury to David Bairstow left no alternative but to play Paul Downton as wicket-keeper — although I had a feeling he would have played anyway once three spinners had been selected — which left room for only two seamers plus the captain. Again Graham Dilley and Graham Stevenson both needed a long work out, Chris Old having dropped into a line and length right from the start of the tour.

The big disappointment was finding that the opening Trinidad attack was just a gentle medium pace. So gentle with Larry Gomes, the former Middlesex player opening the bowling, that nobody on the England side bothered to wear a crash helmet yet we all knew that would be the first item of equipment we would pack in our cricketing bags for the Test.

The second disappointment was the wicket itself. It had been relaid only a couple of months before, used for the first time only four weeks earlier and did not contain one single blade of grass. Looking at the surrounds was even more astonishing. There is only room for three wickets on the square at the most and either side of the wicket for the Trinidad game was just a long stretch of uneven mud. We knew the Test wicket was in there somewhere but nobody had a clue where to look for it.

The wicket had been relaid in order to give it a little more pace and more even bounce. After our experience, there is obviously still a lot to be done to it before it becomes acceptable. It is still very much a spinner's wicket although the ball turns very slowly which doesn't help the Trinidad spinners. Without any grass on it, I found it quite difficult to bowl on. To help me find my length I can usually sort out a patch of grass, a darker spot perhaps to aim at. The wicket for the Trinidad game was exactly the same from one end to the other without any distinguishing marks.

As a final work out before the Test match, the game was not much help apart from those fortunate enough to have a long bat in the middle to get the feeling that the tour had really started. Yet it provided a fascinating aside in that it enabled us all to have a look at Trinidad's new bowling discovery Harold Joseph, a twenty-three year old who had surprised many of the leading batsmen in the Caribbean since we arrived in the domestic Shell Shield competition. We had heard quite a lot about him before we met him. Some people had described him as another Sonny Ramadhin who had teased England into submission almost thirty years earlier. Others said he was another Johnny Gleeson, the Australian spinner who caused our batsmen trouble on two tours of Australia by being able to 'flick' the ball either way with his fingers. We found Joseph a mixture of both and more.

He was a little unfortunate on meeting us on such a slow wicket which helped us to be able to play him off the pitch on the majority of occasions. On a much faster wicket it must be doubtful whether we would have managed the 355 runs we mustered in our first innings yet he still emerged with figures of 5 for 116 off his 51 overs which is still good going for a spinner.

At the end of our innings which occupied all the second day and a large portion of the third, I still don't think anybody discovered how to read Joseph correctly. He was also helped by bowling most of his overs from the pavilion end which meant he bowled out of a dark background as I gather Willie Rodrigues, the former West Indies and Trinidad leg spinner, used to do. He caused England's batsmen considerable trouble on the 1968 tour of the West Indies.

We were not unduly depressed by the fact that nobody on our side had managed to pick what Joseph was doing. After the match I talked to Viv Richards who had taken a century off Trinidad — and Joseph — a fortnight earlier and he confessed that at the end of his innings of 168 for the Combined Islands in a Shell Shield game he had still no idea which way Joseph was going to turn the ball.

Once the West Indies run out of fast bowlers — and during our tour we discovered about eight who could keep them going for some time — I'm sure Joseph will make the grade in Test cricket if given the opportunity. He bowls practically anything. He turns the ball both ways with his wrist spinners and turns the ball both ways with his finger spin. He is very hard to read and we discovered why afterwards especially with his finger spin. Apparently it is all done with his thumb which is carefully hidden from the batsman. He has the ability to make this thumb work backwards so that he can produce a leg spinner — one that breaks from leg to the offside — when he looks as though he is bowling orthodox off spinners, as Graham Gooch found out.

It didn't take Trinidad captain Deryck Murray long to bring his spinners into the attack. After only eight overs in fact, eight overs from Alec Burns and Gomes which Boycott and Gooch had negotiated without the slightest alarm. Off spinner Ranjie Nanan, who went to Pakistan three months earlier on the West Indies tour as understudy to Derek Parry, was the first on. Left arm wrist spinner Alston Daniel, whom we had met in the first match in Pointe-a-Pierre was next followed by Joseph. By that time Gooch had become well established and he walked down the wicket to Boycott and said 'I think I'll play him as an off spinner and see how that works out.' It almost did not because the first ball Gooch received pitched leg stump and went over middle and off.

We knew we were in for a difficult time against him by the way Boycott and Gooch played him. There is probably not a better player of spin bowling in the world today than Boycott. And I know to my cost when bowling my off spin for Northants against Essex that Gooch loves nothing better than to give the slower bowlers a bit of stick. Yet Boycott treated Joseph with the greatest respect and Gooch played one of the most sedate innings I can remember considering there were spinners around. It's difficult trying to hit a spinner out of sight when you haven't a clue which way he was turning the ball.

Both were beaten a few times. Both survived, very conscious of the fact that this would be their last opportunity to get practice in the middle before the Test match. It meant the rest of us had to sit and wait patiently while they added 173 for the first wicket before Boycott was beaten by Joseph — one he later confessed he knew little about — and was bowled.

Their partnership had taken them just three hours which was worth almost a run a minute, most of the stick being handed out to Nanan and Daniel. It was around that time that Nanan was being selected in the West Indies thirteen for the first Test by their selectors who were meeting in Grenada where the Combined Islands were playing Guyana and preparing to lift the Shell Shield trophy for the first time. Those selectors could not have been too happy about their choice the following morning when they read that Nanan's two wickets against us had cost him 116 runs off 43 overs. Daniel's performance confirmed the first impression we had of him in Pointe-a-Pierre. Being a left arm wrist spinner who bowls 'chinamen' — the left arm wrist spinner's googly — he is a bit of a rare bird but he doesn't spin the ball enough to be truly effective on Caribbean wickets.

Joseph claimed the next wicket too, when he had Brian Rose caught behind attempting to cut before Nanan got into the act for the first time. Gooch had been at the wicket for three hours forty minutes hitting three sixes and eight fours when he went back on to his wicket and was bowled by one which kept low. England's next dismissal was particularly unfortunate for the victim Dusty Miller. David Gower offered a fierce return chance to Joseph when he was forced to adjust his shot at the last moment. It was far too hot for Joseph to handle but the ball spun out of his fingers on to the wicket at at the bowler's end and Dusty was run-out, still not having regained his ground when backing up.

With our captain facing only four deliveries before he was caught behind attempting to cut the left arm wrist spinner Daniel, that let me in shortly before the close of play, my first real chance to play a sensible innings of the tour. It was not the ideal time to go to the wicket because it meant that I had to play myself in twice, once that evening and again the following morning.

I was fortunate, however, in that Joseph was undoubtedly tired by the time he attempted to pit his wits against mine. Every player has to make up his own mind how he intends to play a 'mystery' man and I decided that the wicket was slow enough for me to wait until the ball had pitched before making up my mind which way it was going and how I was going to counter it. I must confess now that I still haven't a clue what Joseph was bowling at me except that his length was sometimes a little awry that first evening — as happens with most bowlers of his type until they have more experience — and I was able to pick up a few runs against him without any undue alarms.

David Gower was also playing him well that evening, as he was against any bowler Deryck Murray tried against him. He had made 40 not out by the close. I was on 12 and England were handily placed on 275 for 5. The following morning was a different story.

For a start David's timing deserted him completely. Try as he could, he couldn't get the ball through the field and was almost an hour over his first two runs of the day. He might easily have been out too, when he attempted a drive against opening bowler Burns but Arneuil Rajah dropped the chance in the covers. Then Joseph was set into action again and took the first three wickets to fall.

I was his first victim. I had taken my score to 28 and was feeling good when he bowled what I thought was a low full toss. I tried to whip it away through mid-wicket but it dipped at the last moment — like a flipper — and I was bowled. Paul Downton was soon to follow, a leg before victim and John Emburey became his deserved fifth victim of the innings when he was caught at slip. It wasn't long before our innings folded. Stevo picked up his second duck of the tour and Gower was last man out, top edging an attempted pull against Daniel to give Nanan a simple catch at deepish mid-on. At least I had experienced a decent amount of time out in the middle. Graham Gooch, Geoff Boycott and David Gower had benefited most from the performance which was exactly what England wanted as they were regarded as our key men in the Tests ahead.

From the end of our innings onwards — just after lunch on the third day — the match deteriorated as a spectacle. This was a great pity because I think it would have been fascinating but for the loss of almost the entire first day. It was certainly a great change to play in a game where spin bowlers were given their head — on both sides. Like the majority of batsmen I find Test cricket something of a bore to play against most countries with a never ending stream of fast bowlers lining up to take a shy at you.

There was a slight chance at the start of the Trinidad innings when Both bowled opening batsman Kenrick Bainey first ball with a full toss and again at the start of the final morning when they lost two wickets quickly that we might have been able to bowl them out and leave ourselves with more batting practice. It wasn't to be. Knowing the wicket wasn't going to offer much help — the turn was so slow and the pace bowlers largely ineffective — it was very difficult to retain the sharp edge needed to perform at the highest level. There was also a great lack of atmosphere in the ground which did not help. It can hold 30,000, the largest Test ground in the Caribbean, but there were seldom more than 2,000 in it each day. Local officials explained that most Trinidadians were saving their money to watch the Test and money was in short supply in any case at that time of the year. With Trinidad's famous Carnival only three weeks away, most people were spending their money on the usual pre-Carnival activities.

At nights the calypso singers were competing against each other, trying to drum up support for their annual contest. Local associations of every kind were staging pre-Carnival fêtes — where the locals spent hours just jumping up and down in a frenzied mass — and any spare cash was being spent on buying last minute additions to Carnival costumes and floats. In addition every steel band in the island was spending hours practising at night in front of their own supporters.

Whatever the reason for the small crowd, we all found it difficult to get going knowing that the match was certain to end in a draw. Especially when Larry Gomes, named on the third day as part of the West Indies squad, used up 280 minutes scoring 75 runs to make sure of his Test place.

By the end of that third day when Trinidad had been batting for almost four hours, we had managed only a couple of wickets. That of Bainey who had had his middle stump knocked back by the first ball he had faced and his opening partner Richard Gabriel who became Both's second victim when given out leg before. In reply they had managed to score 144 runs.

Gomes was well set by then, grim defence mixed with the occasional flurry of activity which brought him eight fours in his long stay. I found his partner Augustine Logie the more interesting player. Apart from their seemingly never ending supply of fast bowlers, the West Indies seemed well equipped for younger batsmen to take over in the near future.

We had already seen Everton Mattis and Jeffrey Dujon in Pointe-a-Pierre and Logie also looked a good bet for the future. He impressed me by the amount of time he appeared to have to play the ball, always a good sign in a player. He batted extremely well on the third evening although he was not to last long on the final morning, reaching for a widish delivery from Gooch and getting caught behind.

With Gomes falling shortly afterwards, teased into going down the wicket against Geoff Miller only to be beaten by the turn, offering a stumping chance which Paul Downton accepted with great glee, we did think in terms of bowling them out and having another two hours or so for batting practice at the end of the day. A character by the name of Theodore Cuffy, aided by Deryck Murray who was out to prove a point to the selectors having been overlooked for the Test side, and Ranjie Nanan quickly changed all that.

In just 72 minutes Cuffy scored 61 entertaining runs before he was yorked middle stump by Graham Stevenson. His record suggested he was very much a hit or miss player. He has been playing the first class game for eleven years, mainly as a middle order batsman yet had scored only two centuries. He reminded me very much of Collis King in his approach, a fine striker of the ball when he connected but I doubt whether those moments come very often in his career. He was a candidate to be yorked for the extravagant way he wound himself up. Stevo produced just the right ball. By the time he had finished however, there was nothing left in the game as Murray and Nanan enjoyed themselves in a seventh wicket stand of 122, Trinidad finishing on 392 for 8 when the end came.

As a dress rehearsal for the Test match to come it was all rather disappointing. I benefited from the last session after tea by which time the seamers had taken off their boots and the three spinners were left to do the work. Deryck Murray provided me with my first wicket when he was well caught by John Emburey via bat and pad. I wasn't quite so satisfied with my second wicket soon after, that of opening bowler Burns. He just missed a perfectly straight ball.

The one difficulty in playing three off spinners in one side is giving each of us enough work to do. In an innings lasting just over nine hours I was given just 20 overs split into three spells which is not enough to find any sort of rhythm. Dusty

Miller and John Emburey fared a little better but not much and I don't think any of us came off the field at the end of the match feeling particularly proud of the way we had performed. I can quite understand the suggestions after the match that we had looked a little ragged in the field. As I said earlier, it was very hard to become motivated in a match where it was obvious from about lunchtime on the second day that it was going to end in a draw and with nobody in the ground to help provide atmosphere.

As far as bowling was concerned Graham Dilley and Graham Stevenson had more to be pleased about than anybody. For the first time on the tour Dilley had been able to let himself go and deserved more than the wicket of Rajah both for the effort he put in and the pace of his bowling. Stevo, too, had impressed me. His line and length had been good enough, in my opinion, to earn consideration for a place in our first Test side but he just missed out.

As it turned out only one change was made for the Test match, Chris Old coming in for his Yorkshire colleague Stevenson. Mike Gatting, who had performed particularly well with the bat in the opening match of the tour, was also added to the eleven who played against Trinidad. He was the one to miss out on the morning of the Test when the final selection was made, much to my surprise. I had assumed that we would field all the batsmen we could taking into account our shortage of practice. I was convinced that the final place rested between Dusty and myself with me being the likely man to stand down. It was quite a relief when Both told me that I was in.

TRINIDAD & TOBAGO *v.* ENGLAND
TRINIDAD, FEBRUARY 7–10

England

G. A. Gooch	b Nanan	117
G. Boycott	b Joseph	70
B. C. Rose	c Murray b Joseph	11
D. I. Gower	c Nanan b Daniel	77
G. Miller	run out	19
*I. T. Botham	c Murray b Daniel	0
P. Willey	b Joseph	28
+P. R. Downton	lbw b Joseph	10
J. E. Emburey	c Gabriel b Joseph	1
G. B. Stevenson	b Nanan	0
G. R. Dilley	not out	15
Extras	b 4, lb 2, w 1	7
Total		355

Fall of wickets: 1—173, 2—201, 3—201, 4—243, 5—243, 6—292, 7—320, 8—324, 9—325.

Bowling: Burns 16—5—33—0; Gomes 7—4—3—0; Nanan 43—9—116—2; Daniel 23.3—5—79—2; Joseph 51—11—116—5; Logie 1—0—1—0.

Trinidad & Tobago

R. S. Gabriel	lbw b Botham	38
K. R. Bainey	b Botham	0
H. A. Gomes	st Downton b Miller	75
A. L. Logie	c Downton b Gooch	30
A. T. Rajah	lbw b Dilley	19
T. Cuffy	b Stevenson	61
*+D.L. Murray	c Emburey b Willey	75
R. Nanan	not out	66
A. G. Burns	b Willey	1
A. T. Daniel	not out	0
Extras	b 2, lb 13, nb 12	27
Total	(eight wickets)	392

Fall of wickets: 1—1, 2—101, 3—148, 4—170, 5—205, 6—266, 7—388, 8—392.
H. J. Joseph did not bat

Bowling: Dilley 21—8—63—1; Botham 16—4—44—2; Emburey 32—11—72—0; Stevenson 17—4—46—1; Miller 25—6—65—1; Willey 20—3—61—2; Gooch 12—6—14—1.

* captain + wicket-keeper

Match drawn

5 PAUL DOWNTON (MIDDLESEX & ENGLAND)

First Test

13–18 February

England's young wicket-keeper makes his first appearance for England in the first Test in Trinidad where the start was delayed because of sabotage to the wicket.

The way the match developed over the five days, just about the only thing wrong with my Test debut in Port of Spain, Trinidad was the ending — England's defeat by an innings of 79 runs. For intrigue, drama and tension to accompany a cricket match played at the highest level, the script for my first appearance for my country could hardly have been bettered; the match had the lot.

There was the mystery saboteur who helped delay the start for more than three hours by digging holes in the wicket on the eve of the game. The runaway start Gordon Greenidge and Desmond Haynes gave the West Indies on the first afternoon, our very spirited fight back on the second day which worried them and then the drama of the last day when our desperate battle for survival was finally overtaken by the four pace bowlers who have helped make the West Indies the champions of every facet of the game over the last five years. As one of the men involved in those last desperate hours, I was very disappointed we did not manage to hold on and save it. Perhaps we should have done.

I had not expected to be involved in the first Test when I arrived in the Caribbean a month earlier. I had hoped that I would get my chance on the tour especially after the frustrating period I had gone through on my first tour for England to Pakistan and New Zealand in 1977–78. I was then only twenty with just a mere handful of first class matches behind me for Kent. I hadn't gone there expecting to replace Bob Taylor at any stage and wasn't surprised when I did not and returned home with some of my confidence having evaporated on a tour I had been sent on with the future in mind. Looking back, I do not think the experience did me a lot of good at the time.

At least on this tour to the West Indies I had arrived knowing I stood a chance of competing having, presumably, been selected on the strength of my appearances for Middlesex during the second half of the summer when I had made runs as an opening batsman as well as kept wicket. At least I wasn't a complete unknown any more. I realised that David Bairstow was considered the number one choice having won the position towards the end of the summer at home but I was also encouraged when it was stressed to us that the Test side would be based on performances in the Caribbean and not past records.

To a large extent I was also helped by the fact that David was hampered by an unfortunate foot injury following our visit to St Vincent which left the selectors with no alternative but to play me in the final Test rehearsal against Trinidad and Tobago. Although I never had the opportunity to display any outstanding works of art during the match — the stumping I achieved against Larry Gomes in the game was fairly straightforward once Geoff Miller had lured the batsmen into error — I was reasonably satisfied with my performance.

If very little came my way to provide me with opportunities to increase my number of victims, at least I had not missed anything, had gathered most things cleanly felt I was moving into position smoothly enough although the lack of bounce in the wicket for that match had proved a little awkward. Throughout the match I was conscious that I was being watched very closely and knew I could not afford to make any mistakes because David's foot injury had healed and he was available for selection by the time the team was chosen.

Bob Willis, the tour vice captain until he was forced to return home with a knee injury immediately after the Trinidad Test, was the first to tell me I was playing following the net session at the Queen's Park Oval two days before match started. My selection was confirmed at a team meeting that afternoon before we went off to a West Indies Cricket Board of Control dinner. Normally it is the type of honour you want to shout about but we were all told to say nothing because the team was not being released officially until the next morning. Somehow the news got out because I was congratulated by several of the English pressmen before the dinner started. It was a little awkward not being able to say a word in reply. Fortunately they all understood my predicament.

All sorts of things were going through my head that night and the following morning. I thought of the times I had watched Bob Taylor, Alan Knott and David Bairstow keep wicket for England and how I had been left with an impression that they had been perfect in everything they had done. I knew that I was going to be judged by their standards. It was quite a frightening thought. Above all I wanted to get on with the match so that I could put any thoughts out of my head and become involved in the action. My patience was to be tested.

After all the rain interruptions of the previous two weeks none of us was in the state we would have liked to have been in for a Test match. Geoff Boycott had played four longish innings in the middle but that was not sufficient to satisfy him. David Gower had played two long innings. Graham Gooch had played one, making the century against Trinidad and Tobago in his one and only first class innings of the tour. I had played only one first class match. That had been against Trinidad and Tobago. My stay at the wicket had been short. The bowlers had had only one real opportunity to stretch themselves. That had also been against Trinidad and Tobago and it was not surprising that the final Test side showed only one change from that match with Chris Old coming in for his Yorkshire colleague Graham Stevenson. Personally, with our shortage of batting practice, I was a little surprised that Mike Gatting was the player to be omitted. Mike is a very spirited player, a real fighter but the tour selectors opted for the extra off spinner instead. It was some time before they were forced to make that decision after the events of the first morning.

It had rained the previous day and early in the morning. By the time we arrived at the ground some ninety minutes before the scheduled start, the sun had been shining for three hours or so but there was still a large wet patch behind the wicket at one end where a tap on the Queen's Park Oval watering system had leaked. It was half way through the run up of a fast bowler, just where a wicket-keeper would be trying to keep his feet when standing back. When we examined it, our feet sank in more than a quarter of an inch. Ian Botham described it later as a 'swamp area'. It was an apt description. We were also mystified to see several damp areas on the wicket itself. One was a largish patch about two feet by three feet half way down with three or four other spots about the size of a man's hand. All were too wet to prevent the match starting on time even if that 'swamp' area had not been in existence. It was not until some hours later that we were to discover that these damp patches had been caused by hasty repairs to the wicket after the work of the saboteur who had slashed his way through the covers before crawling underneath to damage the pitch itself.

There was a great deal of resentment felt by certain people in Trinidad because Deryck Murray had again been overlooked by the West Indies selectors for the wicket-keeping role, his position being occupied by Barbadian David Murray who had been the first choice wicket-keeper on the tour to Pakistan at the end of 1980. Deryck is Trinidad's captain and they were proud of his record on the island. His omission had prompted the start of a campaign calling on Trinidadians to boycott the Test match. Steve Cobham, secretary of the Queen's Park Club had also received anonymous telephone calls threatening to damage the wicket and had ordered additional security for the three days immediately before the match.

This involved extra security patrols at night plus the erection of a spotlight to light up the wicket throughout the night. The saboteur — or saboteurs — had done their homework before they struck. On the night before the match the extra patrol failed to arrive and the spotlight failed to work. The pitch digging operation went on undetected.

It all helped to add to the air of unreality on the first morning. It was a rather unsettling period. There were twenty-two cricketers just waiting to get involved but none of us could concentrate our thoughts on the match because none of us knew what was happening and what sort of role we could expect to play at the start. I was down to bat at number eight in the England batting order and I did not know whether I had more time to spend relaxing, soaking up the atmosphere before concentrating my thoughts on batting or whether I would be plunged straight into the action if England were in the field.

None of us was helped either when a few bottles and cans were thrown on to the outfield as the captains went out to toss up. By then the crowd, rather starved of information as to why the start had been delayed until mid afternoon, had grown restless sitting in the hot sun and, for a minute or two, we wondered whether we were in for a riot, not an uncommon event in Test matches in the West Indies. When a start was ordered by the umpires, neither Ian nor Clive Lloyd thought the conditions were fit. The 'swamp' area was still sticky and the repaired areas on the wicket itself were still damp — the main cause of concern. Nobody was sure how the ball would react if it pitched on one of the damp patches.

Those patches were a major influence behind Both's decision to put the West Indies in when he won the toss. Clive told us later he would have done the same thing. As it happened, the ball did very little when it hit those patches except to come through faster. I could really feel the impact through my gloves. But that was all. I had been a little worried before the start on how I would cope after the experience of the Trinidad and Tobago match when the bounce was sometimes very low and the wicket was slow. In those situations it is a little awkward to judge the correct distance to stand. In the Test on that first afternoon, it came through at a pretty even height.

After sitting around for three hours or more, it was a great relief to get started, to know what we were doing. I could concentrate my thoughts on keeping wicket, the adrenalin started to flow. By the end of the day I was feeling confident. I was worried just a couple of times when John Emburey came on to bowl. In his third over a couple drifted down the leg side, the ball shielded for a moment by the body of the batsman. I stopped them but did not gather them cleanly. But, on the whole, I felt I was taking the ball well, moving into the right positions.

More than half the day had been lost. The rest of it belonged to the West Indian openers Haynes and Greenidge who put on 144 before the close although I felt we had bowled well. Graham Dilley was extremely unlucky not to get a nick now and again. Both came charging through the swamp and there was a worry that his back might not have been one hundred per cent. He had felt a twinge or two in the nets a couple of days before but I could tell immediately that it was all there. Chris Old also bowled a very good line, just outside the off stump and we knew John Emburey was going to be in for a long session when he was brought into the attack after just 13 overs. If none of them threatened to run through the West Indies side on that first day, none gave anything away. Yet, at the end of our first 44 overs, the West Indies were 144 without loss, no doubt thinking in terms of 550 plus as a first innings total. Normally Greenidge would outscore Haynes. That day they went along side by side finishing 70 and 68 respectively.

They were fascinating to watch at work together from close quarters; rather frightening too. They both impressed me by the speed in which they picked up the short ball and hooked or cut it. Dilley bowled one to Haynes that was only just short of a length but he was on it in a flash, hooking it for four. In another over Greenidge pulled Dilley for four just in front of square leg and then cover drove the next ball to the boundary. Both were ferocious strokes.

We all knew at the end of that first day we were up against it but the way we clawed our way back into the game on the second day was a sheer delight. We knew we could not afford to give anything away. We didn't. We knew we had to frustrate them, keep them short of runs, force them to make their own errors otherwise all would be lost. We did exactly that. Taking seven West Indian wickets in a full six hour day in exchange for only 221 runs was a high class performance.

Greenidge and Haynes were obviously keen to build quickly on their start of the previous day. They were denied the opportunity with Dilley and Botham at one end, Emburey at the other. Not even Viv Richards was allowed to escape. It took us fifty minutes to achieve that first breakthrough but they had been limited to just 24 runs in that time. Greenidge's patience was, I'm sure, wearing a little thin when he attempted to break loose by hitting Emburey over the top only to loft the ball to our captain at deep mid on when he mistimed his drive.

That let in Viv. My one great memory of the summer at home against the West Indies was of Viv marching to the wicket and starting each innings with a series of fours against our faster bowlers. He came in at Trinidad to find a spinner in the attack and I believe that inhibited him. He played a very chancy stroke against the first delivery he faced against Emburey, going a long way across his wicket to squeeze the ball off his middle stump down towards fine leg for a single. If he was inhibited then, he became even more circumspect when he started to lose partners. The first, Haynes, sent back after a marvellous piece of cricket when he was just four runs short of his century.

The delivery from Emburey was respectable enough without being anything special. The stroke from Haynes was a good one as he attempted to drive. What happened next was remarkable. John Emburey is a tall man which adds to the problems of getting down low. He was also off balance at the end of his delivery, veering slightly to his left. Yet he managed to throw himself full length to his right to take a return catch just inches off the ground. Haynes' century should have been at the end of that stroke. Instead he was walking back to the pavilion.

The timing of that wicket couldn't have been better with Everton Mattis, the young Jamaican making his Test debut, arriving at the wicket. It was just before lunch. After our success of the morning session, Both could afford to apply all the pressure he wanted. Five men ringed the bat but Mattis — whose calmness when all the wickets had been falling around him in the one day international had been impressive — played the first three balls confidently enough. The fourth brought about his downfall. It was a little shorter, a little faster and bounced just a little more to catch him by surprise. He did not quite get on top of it sufficiently to keep it down as Dusty Miller took a good catch, very fine at backward short leg. The West Indies had lost three wickets in the morning for the addition of 60 runs. The pressure was now on them.

The team were feeling very happy. And so was I. I like to break my performances down to 10 over spells. Get through the first 10 overs feeling content and confident and that will spur me on for the next 10. My one concern was being able to concentrate fully on the task knowing that we faced one and a half — possibly two — days in the field. Ken Barrington, our assistant manager, offered a useful tip. He reminded me that we had a drink interval every hour and told me to split the day into six one hour periods and not just three sessions. Get through the first session, settle down for the next. I also found the tempo of Test cricket helped. Vital one day matches for Middlesex had been my most important occasions until then, matches where everything is played at a hectic pace with little time to think. In Tests the tempo is much slower which presents you with the opportunity to think clinically about what you are doing even if the tension is greater.

In his seventy minutes at the crease before lunch Viv had been limited to 18 runs. He was to make only another 11 before he fell. Both made a great fuss about setting his leg side field when Viv came up against Dusty. A six-three field, the six on the leg side placed with great accuracy as if to say to Viv that he couldn't get a ball through. He does tend to play rather uppishly through the mid wicket area, his placement of strokes so perfect he can usually get away with it. That afternoon he failed. Dusty will say it wasn't among the best balls he has bowled. A little short, somewhat inviting but Viv found David Gower's hands at square leg with uncanny accuracy. In just over two hours at the crease he had made only 29 runs, probably one of his slowest ever Test innings.

That brought Clive Lloyd in to join Larry Gomes. Two left handers and I feel more uncomfortable keeping when they are at the wicket than right handers. Probably because I come across many more right handers. You slip easily into a groove. Suddenly everything has to change and the angle is much wider, too. I also knew I had to summon every ounce of concentration. I had stumped Gomes in the Trinidad match and he could present me with another chance. Clive also has a habit of playing almost a walking shot, going well forward and I thought he might give me an opportunity.

The pressure was on them both. Larry because he was the local hero and needed to do well in front of his fellow Trinidadians. Clive because the West Indies were stumbling a little. Clive survived, not without a great deal of difficulty especially against Dilley with the new ball. I think the pressure got to Larry in the end. He was stuck on five for more than an hour when he presented me with my first Test wicket. It was a relatively simple catch. A fairly wide ball from Chris Old which he reached for, got an edge and that was that. As I said, relatively simple — but a nice one to have for all that.

We thought we might have got another soon after. David Murray the 'villain' of the plot having gained preference over Trinidad's Deryck Murray, was on two when we thought we had him taken at short leg off bat and pad. Umpire Douglas Sang Hue thought otherwise and he stayed to help his captain add 75 priceless runs for the seventh wicket.

Both were to fall before the close to leave us content enough on our rest day — brought forward one day because of a pre-Carnival steel band contest taking place on Trinidad's famous Savannah. Even cricket in the West Indies cannot afford to clash with a Carnival event. Murray was four short of his half century when he was taken by a fine running catch at wide mid on hitting against Emburey who also accounted to Clive Lloyd to give him five wickets in the day. Emburey bowled it a little faster than normal Clive tried to turn it on the leg side but ended up playing around it and over it to be bowled.

The end of the West Indies on the third morning was quite spectacular. On the rest day Clive Lloyd had said he wanted 400 runs on the board, another 35 runs from his remaining three wickets. He got them for the loss of Holding and Garner who both fell leg before against Both, a signal for Andy Roberts to hit out boldly. He did, against Both in particular, producing a number of stunning blows in one over, hitting three sixes and a four before reaching his half century, the moment Lloyd chose to declare with 426 runs on the board.

Our immediate target was to score 227 to avoid the possibility of being asked to follow on. We never made it despite a three hour innings from Graham Gooch, the efforts of

David Gower and Geoff Boycott. By the end of that third day we had lost seven wickets scoring 159 runs, mine being the seventh wicket to fall.

Graham demonstrated tremendous character during his stay. He was beaten time and again — the first five balls from one over against Colin Croft — yet put each false stroke behind him and concentrated fully on the next ball. Boycott looked fully in command, timing his strokes beautifully, scoring at a fast rate until he fell immediately after lunch, deceived by the angle of Croft's delivery. He is awkward to combat. He bowls from the very edge of the return crease and also leans well over to his left side, making the angle even more difficult. It's very easy to forget exactly where your off stump is when facing him. Geoff had his covered when he went to drive but the ball cut away just enough to find the edge to offer Viv Richards the sort of chance he seldom misses even though it travelled to him quickly at third slip.

His is still the wicket the opposition seem to prize more than any other. The sight of him retreating into the pavilion inspired them even more. There was quite a procession of batsmen going backward and forward before I was called upon. Brian Rose, whose confidence could not have been high going into the match after his rather unfortunate start to the tour, was taken at short leg before Roberts ended Gooch's three hour ordeal with a ball which cut back quite a lot.

Dusty Miller never had a chance to settle before he was beaten by Croft's angle of delivery, Both was given out leg before for a duck — his second on the ground — which some thought might have been going down the leg side and Peter Willey was leg before to a yorker from Garner. He must be the best bowler of a yorker in the world, very difficult to pick up accurately from the height he delivers the ball. He had bowled three others to Willey in that over.

It was my turn then to join David Gower who had looked completely at home, playing very straight and without apparent difficulty. I had hoped to last to the end of the day but fell shortly before the close, beaten by Larry Gomes of all bowlers. Michael Holding bowled the first ball I received in Test cricket. I didn't pick the first one up very well after watching his lovely, rhythmic approach to the wicket. I felt better about the second one, a little shorter which got up but I managed to play it down. I also got two runs off him the following over, a little uppishly through mid-wicket but nowhere near the fielders. I was to get only two more before Clive turned to the off spin of Richards and Gomes to speed up the arrival of the new ball the following morning. I much prefer to face the faster bowlers when I am still settling down at the wicket. Seeing Gomes bowling was a surprise, especially Gomes bowling off spin. I'm not too sure now what happened to the one which got me. I think I must have played inside it. Nobody in Trinidad could have cared less that night. Their man had taken a wicket. That was all that mattered. I wasn't so enthusiastic about the achievement.

By the close of the third day we were still 68 runs from avoiding the follow on with three wickets left and the new ball just a few overs away. David Gower remained our only hope after the way he had batted but when he fell leg before to Croft early on the fourth morning the only other thing we achieved was forcing Clive to call for the new ball to finish our innings.

Rain had also delayed our ending, starting to fall the minute David Gower reached the pavilion. It also delayed the start of our battle for survival but not long enough as it turned out. In the two hours forty minutes remaining that day we were to lose Gooch and Rose to Michael Holding, bowling faster than he had done at any stage in the match before yet we were also encouraged by the way Gower joined Boycott in a 40 run partnership for the third wicket.

Holding had been the only West Indies fast bowler not to take a wicket in the first innings. That obviously spurred him on. There was also a race between him and Croft to reach one hundred wickets. Croft's five in the first innings had taken his total to ninety-nine in his twenty-first Test. Holding had started our second innings on ninety-eight — and soon got the two he needed having Gooch leg before and seeing Rose caught behind.

I still thought we could save the match when the final day started, a day in which twenty minutes were lost at the start because the Queen's Park Oval ground staff had been slow in preparing the wicket much to Clive Lloyd's great annoyance. The weather was also threatening to help, the Northern Range of mountains which form a backcloth to the ground on the opposite end to the pavilion, often being completely shrouded as rain swept down the slopes. Not sufficient was to fall on the ground itself to help our cause.

We started that last day needing another 183 runs to make the West Indies bat again. We knew that wasn't on. Our only objective was to still be batting at the close. With the new ball not being due until mid-afternoon we desperately needed to survive the two hour pre-lunch session without the West Indies inflicting too much damage. Instead we were to lose two wickets. Gower was caught behind down the leg side attempting a leg glance against Roberts while Croft obtained his one hundredth Test victim when he had Miller edging a catch to third slip. We needed Both and Boycott then to take us through most of the afternoon and see the shine off the new ball. It wasn't to be.

For an hour it appeared they would be able to do it. Both curbed his natural attacking instincts and played with great tact. I thought Boycott was superb. He will say he has played better during his eighteen year career but that was the best I had seen him play. He looked capable of playing forever not having to think too seriously about scoring runs although he never missed an opportunity. We had long recognised he was our main hope and I believe Clive had resigned himself to the new ball of being his only hope of getting him out. Before then, however, Both was to get himself out.

Gomes and Richards were in action again, brought on to hurry through the overs before Clive had his final fling. The new ball was four overs away when Both could not resist having one go at Viv and skied a catch straight to Holding at long on. It will be a stroke he will regret for a long time, the first turning point. The second came with the new ball itself, the second over with it when Holding produced a brutish delivery which flew off the shoulder of Boycott's bat to third slip and ended his five and a quarter hour stay.

His departure let me in to join Peter Willey with rain about to fall. It came down heavily at times, enough to force us off the field if the match had been in England yet I wasn't too concerned. Having worked myself up into the right frame of mind for the battle, with Willey playing well, we were more concerned about having our concentration broken by having to go off the field than the rain itself. I felt remarkably comfortable despite the new ball. I can't remember playing and missing as we tried to eat into the time left. The only occasion I felt bothered was when Holding went off a short run and bowled me a short ball. He isn't much slower off his short run and is far more difficult to pick up.

Eventually the rain became so heavy we were forced off. With the tea interval as well, more than half an hour went by before we got back on the field. As I feared, the break did not help. I had not really settled in again when I was caught at first slip off Roberts. It was a good ball, fairly straight but then it started to drift away in the air and I got the nick the West Indies wanted. I was very disappointed about getting out. I felt at the time I could have stayed there and done the necessary for England.

The end wasn't far away. Roberts bowled Emburey, Willey fell in a similar way to me, this time against Garner who needed just one more delivery to take the final wicket of Chris Old just before the last 20 overs were due to start, the dark, threatening clouds having lifted to ease the pressure on the West Indies bowlers.

With our shortage of practice — especially against pace bowling — before the Test started, we did not bat as well as we would normally have done. I thought we should have saved it on that last day against an attack which was getting tired even though Lloyd — with four fast men to play with — can ease the demands made on them. Yet a fascinating match to remember on my first appearance for England, disappointed as we all were at the end of it on a wicket which was supposed to have presented us with our best chance of a victory in the Caribbean.

WEST INDIES *v.* ENGLAND (First Test) TRINIDAD, FEBRUARY 13–18

West Indies		
C. G. Greenidge	c Botham b Emburey	84
D. L. Haynes	c and b Emburey	96
I. V. A. Richards	c Gower b Miller	29
E. Mattis	c Miller b Emburey	0
H. A. Gomes	c Downton b Old	5
*C. H. Lloyd	b Emburey	64
+D. A. Murray	c Botham b Emburey	46
A. M. E. Roberts	not out	
M. E. Holding	lbw b Botham	26
J. Garner	lbw b Botham	4
C. E. H. Croft	not out	4
Extras	lb 15, nb 3	18
Total	(nine wickets dec.)	426

Fall of wickets: 1–168, 2–203, 3–203, 4–215, 5–257, 6–332, 7–348, 8–383, 9–393

Bowling: First innings – Dilley 28–4–73–0; Botham 28–6–113–2; Old 16–3–49–1; Emburey 52–16–124–5; Miller 18–4–42–1; Gooch 2–0–3–0; Willey 3–1–4–0.

England				
G. A. Gooch	b Roberts	41	lbw b Holding	5
G. Boycott	c Richards b Croft	30	c Haynes b Holding	70
B. C. Rose	c Haynes b Garner	10	c Murray b Holding	5
D. I. Gower	lbw b Croft	48	c Murray b Roberts	27
G. Miller	c Murray b Croft	3	c Greenidge b Croft	8
*I. T. Botham	lbw b Croft	0	c Holding b Richards	16
P. Willey	lbw b Garner	13	c Lloyd b Garner	21
+P. R. Downton	b Gomes	4	c Lloyd b Roberts	5
J. E. Emburey	not out	17	b Roberts	1
G. R. Dilley	b Croft	0	not out	1
C. M. Old	b Roberts	1	c sub b Garner	0
Extras	b 4, lb 4, nb 3	11	b 1, lb 3, nb 6	10
Total		178		169

Fall of wickets: 1–45, 2–63, 3–110, 4–121, 5–127, 6–143, 7–151, 8–163, 9–167. 1–19, 2–25, 3–86, 4–103, 5–134, 6–142, 7–163, 8–167, 9–169

Bowling: First innings – Roberts 13–3–41–2; Holding 11–3–29–0; Croft 22–6–40–5; Garner 23–8–37–2; Richards 7–2–16–0; Gomes 2–1–4–1. Second innings – Holding 18–6–38–3; Roberts 21–7–41–3; Garner 25–10–31–2; Croft 16–5–26–1; Richards 10–6–9–1; Gomes 9–4–14–0

West Indies won by an innings and 79 runs

6 BOB WILLIS (WARWICKSHIRE & ENGLAND VICE-CAPTAIN)

For the England vice-captain the tour was to prove disastrously short and Bob Willis tells of his disappointment of hopes unfulfilled.

It's all so vastly different when you are the victim and not just the bystander. I should have been accustomed to the farewell scenes of players being sent home early when my turn came in Trinidad. After all I had been given my first Test chance by flying out to Australia to join Ray Illingworth's side in 1970/71 as an injury replacement when Alan Ward broke down. On most of my tours abroad since then I'd waved goodbye to players. Even helped to make that return home decision when I had been vice captain. Such occasions had never been pleasant.

When it happened to me I felt desperate. Part of me was ready for home by then. There is so little to do in the West Indies when you are not playing cricket that I found it easy to become bored. And I hadn't been playing cricket. Then there was that big feeling of disappointment of not being able to carry through the job I had been given. Not being able to help the rest of the players faced with the enormous task of trying to put one over against the most fearsome side the West Indies had ever produced even if it wasn't so attractive to watch as the sides led by Sir Frank Worrell and Sir Gary Sobers.

There was so much I felt I could have done — like helping Graham Dilley. He is a quiet lad, a little lacking in self confidence which is perhaps understandable at his age but who looked a genuine Test fast bowler the way he rushed in at Trinidad during the West Indies innings. He has it in him to be as quick as anything the West Indies possess and I was looking forward to bowling with him, helping to bring him out and putting him on the right lines.

There was skipper Ian Botham as well. Captaincy is still a comparatively new thing for him and he needed help on the field so that he was not burdened with making all the decisions. He needed somebody to turn to for a word of advice or confirmation that he was doing the right thing, making the right decisions. That should have been my role. I wasn't in a position to carry it on.

And then there was the battle of wits against the West Indies, probing their weaknesses, learning about their strengths, attempting to find ways of combating their fast bowling squad which now works like a well oiled machine. Each one knows what he is doing. Michael Holding, Andy Roberts, Joel Garner and Colin Croft are all highly intelligent cricketers who have worked out the weaknesses of the batsmen they come across and play on those weaknesses.

I saw it as part of my role to study the weaknesses of the West Indies batting line-up, try and expose them and help the other bowlers exploit them. Before the first Test in Trinidad I had stressed the need to make sure that we did everything we could to frustrate Viv Richards at the start of his innings, make sure that he was never given an easy run and was kept on a tight rein the whole time. Ian and the other bowlers did a magnificent job in keeping him in check with a more defensive field than we might otherwise have employed against him and it gave me a great deal of satisfaction in seeing Viv out for only 29 after more than two hours at the wicket. There was a touch of desperation about the shot he played which resulted in him being caught at square leg off Geoff Miller.

These were the sort of things I knew I would be missing when it was decided my right knee would not heal in time for me to play a useful part on the tour as a bowler. There was some talk of my staying on, almost in an advisory capacity to help Ian with the task of running the side but I knew the decision to go back to England was the right one.

I was already feeling sorry for myself by then. By nature I'm a bit of a pessimist and I needed to return to give myself a mental boost by making sure my knee was examined and treated by the specialist in Warwickshire who had been tending it with loving care for the previous five years.

I had a responsibility to England. I also had a greater responsibility to myself, my wife and my whole future beyond my cricket playing days. As Ken Barrington said to me 'Don't forget Bob, you'll need that right leg to walk around on for another forty years to come.'

I had set out for the West Indies with such high hopes in January. My summer had been a troubled one at home, softened by the pleasure of being able to lead Warwickshire to the John Player League title in my first season as county captain. But the Test match scene had turned a little sour for me.

Not being able to clinch victory in the first Test against the West Indies at Trent Bridge had been a bitter disappointment. I had been pleased with the way I had bowled especially after being written off by so many cricket writers following the tour to Australia. I thought we had nailed them on the final day at Trent Bridge only to lose the Test match by two wickets. I was so disappointed that I had to walk away from the final ceremonies in front of the Nottinghamshire pavilion when all the presentations were being held. Defeat leaves me completely drained especially at that level.

From then on the summer had not gone my way as far as England was concerned. I had a little trouble with my knees, lost my bowling rhythm to such an extent that I virtually talked myself out of a Test place by mid summer. I was bowling rubbish and I knew it.

The end of season break before the start of the West Indies tour had been a relief. A chance to get myself together mentally and physically, boosted by the knowledge I had come through the pre-tour medical satisfactorily. Everything was set for the Caribbean and I looked forward to the role I was to play for England, utilising my experience from eight previous tours abroad including a previous visit to the West Indies under Mike Denness in 1974.

Almost from the start things began to go wrong. Looking at the tour programme it seemed the only match Ian Botham could have off before the round of Test matches started was the second game against the Windward Islands in St Vincent. It was decided that he should lead the side in the opening fixture — part of cricket's tradition that the tour captain should play in the first game — while I trained and took over the captaincy for the second game.

Rain in St Vincent caused us to change our plans drastically. With the four day match against the Windward Islands washed out to be replaced by two one day fixtures, it was essential Ian should play to keep in practice. There were no other net facilities available.

By the time the first one day match against the Windward Islands started, I was also badly in need of match practice. I had done my share in the nets in Trinidad while the team had been playing in Pointe-a-Pierre but nothing can compare with actually bowling in the middle.

My rustiness was apparent with the first ball I bowled — or rather didn't bowl. It slipped out of the back of my hand as I was bringing my arm over to deliver causing David Gower at extra cover to take swift evasive action while the batsman wondered what was happening. It must have been the widest delivery ever recorded in cricket history when the umpire decided to interpret that ball as a genuine delivery.

To help me get my rhythm going and my run up sorted out, it was decided that I should bowl my eight overs full out rather than split them in half which is the normal pattern in one day cricket for a fast bowler. I never made those eight overs.

Half way through the seventh I felt my right knee jar as my foot found one of the many holes in the St Vincent outfield. I managed to complete the rest of the over before walking out of the game. I didn't realise at the time that I was walking out of the tour.

My hours — days even — of agony, torment and complete frustration were about to begin. Originally I thought I might be fit enough to play in the opening one day international on the same ground. The following day when I woke up and found the knee still painful, I knew I had no chance.

My next target was the match against Trinidad in Port of Spain. But that came and went without my even having a genuine bowl in the nets. Not only was the knee still painful but it would have been silly to have attempted to bowl in the Trinidad nets which were never ready in time when we required them and the run-ups were in such a poor state that it was impossible for a completely fit bowler to turn his arm over as he wanted to. They were full of holes and ruts and one further jar on that knee might have been the end for me for good.

The first course of treatment I had did not work either and I soon had to face up to the fact that there was no way I was going to be fit for the First Test. Guyana was my next objective.

The next course of treatment proved very painful. An injection right into the knee which caused quite a violent reaction but I was encouraged by the fact that it hurt so much. The specialist in Port of Spain suggested that the violent reaction meant he had hit the cause of the trouble. I was able to relax more than I had done previously on the tour, even getting eight hours sleep a night without having to listen to therapy tapes I always carry around with me. I relaxed listening to my favourite Bob Dylan instead.

I had spent most of the match against Trinidad watching the game from a seat high in the Queen's Park Oval pavilion right behind the bowler's arm so that I could see what our bowlers were doing wrong and help to put things right. Even though I wasn't playing in that First Test match, I felt that I had some constructive criticisms to make which must have helped. I was delighted with the way Graham Dilley, Chris Old, Ian Botham and John Emburey bowled especially on that second day when we managed to take seven West Indies wickets in exchange for 221 runs. I would have settled for that return every day.

My main enemy was boredom. Waiting for room service or any kind of service in the Hilton Hotel only aggravated the problem. There was little I could do during the day except offer the odd word of advice to the lads and keep their spirits up. Nothing I could do in the evening. It is at times like this that you miss your home and need the comfort of your wife and family. My wife Julia understands me so well. She knows when I need to talk while she listens and offers words of sympathy and understanding and she knows the other mood when she can register the kick in the pants that all players need at some time during their careers.

Although I could not strain the knee in any way, there was also the need to keep myself in shape physically so that I would be ready to return immediately the specialist gave the all clear. The only break in my dull and boring routine came at the close of play when all the players trooped in to taste that special moment together in the dressing room after a day's play. That was the time I was going out to grind my way around the boundary edge of the Queen's Park Oval. Sometimes I would have Roland Butcher or Mike Gatting — neither playing in the Test — for company. Usually I did it alone. I was grateful that the spectators were generally going home and not witnessing my agony.

That was my agony. Nobody could help me. Even worse, I felt so powerless to help the lads on the field in their struggle to stay alive in that First Test. I didn't think we batted particularly well during our first innings but I was full of admiration for the way we tackled the task of trying to save the match on the final day. And for their bowling attack which finally proved too much for us. I readily admit I am not great shakes with the bat and my presence might not have helped during the final session but I was upset that I couldn't get on to the field and try to play my part.

D-Day for me was the day after our innings defeat. A special net session had been arranged for me in the morning to be followed by a visit to the specialist to see if there was any point in my carrying on and being able to play in Guyana. Long before that visit to the specialist, I knew what the verdict was going to be. As soon as I bowled I realised the knee wasn't right.

There was still some time to go before the final decision was made. With a free day on their hands and the last night in Port of Spain to say thank you to the people who had helped and comforted us in Trinidad, most of the players were split up and the decision for me to return to Warwickshire was not going to be released officially until the following morning. But somehow the news spread and the lads still in the hotel threw a farewell party for me. It was a nice gesture.

The big wrench came the following morning when the players were packing and getting ready to fly to Georgetown while I was still wondering the exact nature of my knee trouble and thinking of joining the dole queue as one of the country's unemployed. The players were leaving in mid-morning. My flight home was not until the evening. I felt utterly miserable. There were sympathetic handshakes and words of encouragement from the rest of the lads, the large press corp who travel abroad with us and English supporters who were staying at the hotel. They helped — a little.

It was a lonely ride home although there were a number of people I knew on the flight. My mood was not lifted until my knee was probed by my own specialist at home and he was able to discover the root of the trouble. There was a small foreign body which had to be removed and that was a relief. I had wondered whether the knee injury had been just the result of general wear and tear after years of bowling and that my career might have been over.

Yet I still felt a little guilty. All the time the knee was being probed, the reports were coming back home of the political troubles in Georgetown. I would not have enjoyed Georgetown one bit. I felt for the players. But I was several thousand miles away unable to help and do my bit towards lifting them — the one job I had been specially selected for when I had been named as tour vice captain the previous September.

7 GEOFF MILLER (DERBYSHIRE & ENGLAND)

The successor to Bob Willis as vice-captain tells of the frustrations and disappointments the team faced in Guyana where rain caused the cancellation of the scheduled four day match and the 'Jackman Affair' blew up.

Losing the First Test was sickening enough. Losing Bob Willis twenty-four hours later was even worse. Although I was to benefit within three days when the full tour selection committee back in England appointed me vice-captain in his place.

I was thrilled and honoured. But I wish I had been given the role in any other circumstances. We were packing for our early morning departure for Guyana the following day when the news spread that Bob's right knee injured in St Vincent would not be ready for another month or six weeks.

Bob's importance to the tour both as a personality and as vice-captain can be measured by the fact that there was a strong temptation to keep him on as a non playing advisor. He wished to go back however to get the right treatment on his knee so that he would be fit to lead Warwickshire at the start of the next home season and I think that was the right choice however upset he felt at the time.

I could understand and share his misery. Thirteen months earlier in Australia I had been forced home with a back injury and made an early exit from the tour. Like Bob, I was whisked home just after we had been beaten in the first Test of the series. The rest of the tour was pure agony for me, listening to the ball by ball commentaries on the radio, reading the scores in the papers, seeing the team struggle from so far away but feeling completely helpless to do anything about it. I'm sure Bob shared in the agony of the events to follow as much as he would have done if he had been there.

Before another week had gone by we were to lose Brian Rose as well when it was discovered that he had a slight defect in his right eye which was preventing him picking up the ball as quickly as he should have done in order to score runs or even make catches in the outfield. We had all been at a loss to explain Brian's run of low scores on the tour after the way he had handled the West Indies fast bowlers in the series at home the previous summer. The eye defect explained it all.

Being sent home is a wretched feeling. I was shattered when it happened to me but, looking back, I'm glad that decision was taken. Going back over the years, many players have been forced to return home early from tours and in each case the decision has proved right. The player concerned has been able to get proper treatment from people at home who understand him and his injury and put them right in time to play the following season. The one great trouble with being injured on tour is that you are passed from doctor to doctor, specialist to specialist as you travel around with the team and there is no continuity in the treatment.

I had not given much thought about the vice-captaincy issue until we flew out of Port of Spain, Trinidad and headed for Georgetown, Guyana leaving Bob behind. I certainly did not start considering myself in the running until I learned my name had been linked with the position by the newspapers back home. There were several other candidates such as Brian Rose, Somerset's captain, Chris Old, Yorkshire's new captain and one of the most experienced tourists and Geoff Boycott who had captained England before on tour.

That's why I considered myself fortunate when I was told that I was to take over. And I like to think now that Both and myself were a good combination, almost an ideal combination because we are good for each other in a cricketing sense as well as being able to get along with each other off the field.

We will never approach the game in the same way. We are two entirely different characters for a start and the very nature of the roles we play in the game force us to have a different approach. Ian is a larger than life fellow, big and strong, the type who would have been the first out of the trenches leading the troops if he had been around in the First World War. He's aggressive in his bowling approach believing every ball should take a wicket and the batsman can't play.

As a batsman he loves to smash the ball all around the ground. As a leader in the field he always wants to attack.

My smaller frame prevents me smashing the ball around. As a spin bowler I have to rely more on thinking batsmen out, winning a battle of wits and as a captain I start with a more defensive attitude, more of a wait and see approach rather than go charging in.

Some years ago sitting on the balcony at Chesterfield I discussed my attitude and approach with Ray Illingworth, the former England captain and another off spinner. He agreed with my philosophy which is basically that if I find myself on a flat, unhelpful, wicket I give the opposition nothing. If I find myself on a wicket in my favour I give the opposition nothing and bowl them out.

I suppose somewhere in between Both's approach to cricket and my own outlook on the game would be the ideal road to follow. The important part of our relationship is that we have always managed to get along with each other off the field as well as on. When, after my appointment, I made a suggestion that Both did not agree with and went on his own way I never felt snubbed. That was important.

It was also important that I should understand what Both was trying to do, especially on the field and I had trained myself to do that long before I was given the vice-captaincy. During his days as Derbyshire captain Eddie Barlow, that stocky, aggressive South African all rounder, once asked me what I thought about between overs, even between deliveries on the field. Very little, I told him. He immediately gave me a lecture.

He told me that although at that stage I was just a player, I should still be thinking about the game every moment. I should be acting as a captain in my thoughts, thinking about possible bowling changes, working out why the captain at the time made a bowling change. Think about field placings, study the batsmen to discover his strengths and weaknesses. 'It will also help you to concentrate fully for six hours and make you more prepared to take over the captaincy if you should ever be offered the chance,' he told me. It worked out to be sound advice.

From that moment onwards I did as he said and it certainly

eased the load a little when I took over the Derbyshire captaincy from David Steele in the middle of the 1979 season at home. During the tour of the West Indies I had 'captained' the side in the matches in Pointe-a-Pierre and the two games in Trinidad, including the Test. I knew what Both was trying to do even if I did not agree completely with his views all the time.

I have enjoyed captaining Derbyshire. It has given me a fresh outlook on cricket. It has also given me additional problems to solve, particularly in the field of man management.

I undoubtedly made mistakes in the way I approached some Derbyshire players during my first few months in charge. In fact I know I did but senior Derbyshire players such as Mike Hendrick, Bob Taylor and David Steele helped me out. I was certainly better prepared than I might have been for the man management role I was to encounter as soon as I became vice-captain on the tour and the rain plus the political situation caused havoc with our Georgetown, Guyana section.

Before we went there, we knew it was going to be the most difficult leg. Georgetown has a reputation for violence in the streets and muggings from the 'choke and rob' gangs are part of everyday life. There would be no going out in the evenings to a quiet restaurant, perhaps a stroll around the town or a drink or two in a different hotel bar just to change the scenery. We knew we were going to be confined to our hotel in the evenings. We did not know we were going to be confined there in the afternoons too because of the non stop tropical rain which greeted us on our arrival. It had been raining solidly for three or four days before we arrived and the Bourda test ground, one of the prettiest in the Caribbean, was virtually under water.

Most of Georgetown is below sea level, built on land reclaimed by early Dutch settlers from the sea at the mouth of the Demerara River. The whole town is served by a system of dykes and ditches and the Bourda ground itself is surrounded by a moat six feet wide. The moat was full almost to overflowing and this did not help the drainage from the ground.

The whole visit was most unsettling long before the Robin Jackman Affair became front page news at home and throughout the Caribbean. He had flown in to join us two days after our arrival, just when the rain was easing and hopes were raised that we might be able to play one or two one day games to replace the washed out four day match against Guyana. The sky would brighten during the afternoon which made us start thinking cricket again. Then we would wake up the next morning to find that just a shower was enough to cause another postponement. I played on the Bourda ground in 1972 when I toured the West Indies with England Young Cricketers but never saw the ground last winter. I don't think any of the lads saw it apart from Both who made one early morning inspection.

The main problem facing the manager, assistant manager, Both and myself was how to keep the players occupied, keep them motivated and stop their minds wandering. It became increasingly difficult when we first began to feel the political undertones following Robin's arrival and the suggestions that the tour might be cancelled. We were desperately seeking all the practice facilities we could to keep the party in shape physically but it was hard for them to concentrate, work up enthusiasm for training when there was a chance the only activity they faced was walking up the steps to catch a plane home.

It was especially hard for players such as Mike Gatting, Roland Butcher and David Bairstow who had all missed the Trinidad game and the Test match and were looking forward to playing against Guyana to prove themselves and fight for a place in the Second Test. That chance was denied them.

We did manage to find a sports hall which allowed us to play football while it poured outside although it took some time to find the right formula. By the time we did, the mosquitos had driven us out. Peter Willey and Graham Gooch were the worst to suffer, bitten continually on their legs. After the first day Graham cracked 'I'm going for the world record tomorrow, one hundred bites on one leg.' I don't think he was far off when he finished.

We tried five aside to start with but the court was a little too small. Then we tried four aside and finally three aside. That was the right number for the size of the court but it meant that too many players were left standing around watching. And standing around meant inviting the mosquitos to attack. I did plenty of standing around unfortunately. Assistant manager Ken Barrington was the goalkeeper in my side and I can say without fear of contradiction he was the worst goalkeeper we could have had. Manager Alan Smith showed some neat touches still, as you might expect from a man who won a soccer blue and was on the board of Aston Villa at one time. Ian was also what you might expect as a reserve Fourth Division striker!

Graham Stevenson was the most amusing. He is a fanatic Sheffield Wednesday supporter and spent most of the time standing on the opposition goal-line trying to shoot so that he could do his impersonation of Wednesday's winger Terry Curran.

Back home Graham likes nothing better than to go down to his local pub, have a pint and play snooker. He was given the job of organising a snooker contest but he under-estimated the threat of John Emburey who is another good snooker and darts player. Stevenson was the obvious favourite but gave himself such a handicap that John Emburey walked away with the snooker prize. Stevenson was funny to watch. He doesn't go far without wearing his flat hat and he insisted on wearing it throughout the snooker tournament, racing around the table like an Alex 'Hurricane' Higgins potting the ball. Like the professionals, he was always thinking three or four shots ahead while most of us were content if we hit the ball we were aiming at.

We also organised a gambling horse racing game played with cards. It was about the only time on tour that we got the better of West Indies fast bowler Michael Holding. He was staying in the same hotel and kept popping into our team room to try his luck at horse racing — and popping out again to fetch some more money when he lost.

The nearest we got to playing something resembling cricket for four days was when Ken Barrington discovered a school playground with a fairly flat tarmac surface. It was large enough for us to get some batting practice in but we had to abandon that when we ruined almost every cricket ball we had on the hard surface.

None of us had picked up a bat for seven days by the time

we discovered a dry ground in the Guyana Police Headquarters and managed to stage a one day match between ourselves. Ian led one side, I led the other with some volunteer local cricketers making up the teams. Even that day was tinged with sadness for it was then that we learned that Brian Rose was to return home with his eye defect and that the Guyana Government had started to probe the South African visas in Robin's passport.

Ian's team won fairly comfortably on the best practice facilities we had encountered in the Caribbean. The wicket was lively and the occasion was given atmosphere by a crowd the majority of Fourth Division soccer clubs would have been pleased to see inside their grounds on a Saturday afternoon. There were just a couple of hundred people at the start but they began to turn up in their thousands before lunch when word spread around Georgetown that they could at last see the England team in action. They were a knowledgeable crowd too, ready to applaud the finer points of the game. David Gower and Graham Gooch gave them every opportunity in their respective innings. So did Graham Stevenson with an absolute sizzler of a delivery which took off to find the edge of Geoff Boycott's bat leaving David Bairstow to take a simple catch behind in an all Yorkshire scene.

We blamed 'Colonel' Barrington for our defeat. He had warned us before the start that the game would be played under strict match conditions. Just how strict we discovered when the 'Colonel' acted as umpire and fired out two of my batsmen Roland Butcher and Peter Willey leg before when each had scored two. Willey in particular was not very pleased.

We arranged a match on similar lines in Barbados almost a week later when we were waiting to hear whether the Foreign Ministers of Barbados, Jamaica and Antigua plus the Chief Minister in Montserrat were agreeable to the tour going ahead. I got my revenge in that second match. Helped, I must admit, by the fact that I picked the teams on the second occasion. And I also had the pick of the local cricketers who came along to help. That was a complete accident. As they turned up in the dressing room on the Kensington Oval ground in Bridgetown I just allotted them to one side or the other. I did not have a clue who they were or how good they were. It just happened that the best bowlers finished up on my side and I couldn't convince Both afterwards that I didn't have any prior knowledge.

Throughout that troubled period in Georgetown we all began to appreciate the work load put on the shoulders of manager Alan Smith. I think it is only right that we should all say 'thanks'.

He was always the first to say 'well done' after a particularly fine performance on the field by a player. In Georgetown he received very little sleep, was constantly on the telephone or being called to meetings at the British High Commission to discuss the political situation. He could have quite easily — and justifiably — sought out his hotel room in between these crisis talks to catch up on some rest yet he insisted on turning up at every one of our work-outs to play his full part and throughout the tour proved the most eager of net bowlers.

I know he did have one regret. We found a particularly lively net when we arrived in Bridgetown and the manager is still pretty lively these days. Awkward too with his strange windmill type action which results in him delivering the ball a fraction of a second before you think he is going to. He tried his hardest to get 'Colonel' Barrington on the receiving end in that lively net so that he could drop a couple short 'just to make up for all the times he hammered Warwickshire when I was captain'. The 'Colonel' wasn't having any of it. But those were happier times when the escape from Georgetown had been put behind us.

As I said earlier, I wish I could have taken the vice-captaincy in happier circumstances. And wish I had more to show for my first week in a position of some authority than four rained off days, a practice match between ourselves, a second defeat in the one-day international series and an evacuation of Guyana to help organise. Unfortunately such scenes appear to be coming more commonplace in international cricket these days.

8 DAVID BAIRSTOW (YORKSHIRE & ENGLAND)

Second One Day International, Guyana

26 February

England's wicket-keeper tells of his disappointment with his performance in the match against the Young West Indies XI and at not being selected for the first Test. He goes on to describe the one day international in Guyana.

It was like a scene I had watched several times on television newsreels about the Vietnam war. Two troop carrying helicopters swooping low over the dykes and ditches and open countryside searching for their target before dropping down smoothly in a clearing in the middle of a clump of palm trees.

Within seconds of landing and while the huge rotor blades were still turning, the door slid open and the occupants scrambled out, racing for cover in a crouching run, their weapons at the ready.

The occupants of the helicopters were not troops however. That was us, the England cricket party, arriving at the Albion Sports Ground in Berbice, some eighty-five miles along the coast from Georgetown, Guyana for the second one day international of the tour. It was the highlight of our rain ruined, politically marred week on the South American mainland.

Certainly it was the highlight of the tour for me at that stage after missing out on the first Test in Trinidad following a septic athlete's foot injury I had picked up in St Vincent which stopped me practising for four days at a most vital stage of the tour.

I was perfectly fit by the time the first Test team was selected. I doubt whether I had ever been fitter in my life in fact. I had used the time during the Trinidad match to play extra games of squash with our physiotherapist Bernard Thomas and he also had me chasing up and down the squash courts in short bursts to improve my mobility as well as putting me through a number of tough abdominal exercises. I was bursting to play in that first Test but was left out largely, I was told, on the grounds that Paul Downton had kept in the game against Trinidad and therefore had experienced the wicket conditions.

Whatever the explanation I was still very upset at being left out. For the previous eighteen months I had been selected as England's first choice wicket-keeper for all the one day internationals as I had in the first one day international in St Vincent. But I was eager to prove that I could be just as effective over the longer course of a five day game.

It has always upset me that some people seem to believe that I am just a one day player. I know I'm the boisterous type, considered a little noisy perhaps and aggressive. I enjoy the excitement of sudden death competitions, the spills and thrills of a roundabout and I know people expect things to happen when I march out to the wicket in tight situations.

But, after sixteen years of keeping wicket, starting my Yorkshire cricket career whilst I was still at school, I feel I can do just as good a job in a five day match. I know I can keep wicket and retain my concentration for that length of time. I can also bat stubbornly and stick around in the middle if the match situation demands such an approach.

After being understudy to both Bob Taylor and Alan Knott, I had finally made it and was England's first choice Test wicket-keeper towards the end of the West Indies series at home in 1980 and kept in the Centenary Test against Australia at Lord's. The tour to the West Indies was to be my big chance to show what I could do and establish myself. Yet when that first Test came along I was left sitting on the side as a spectator largely as a result of a foot injury. It was sickening.

I was also annoyed with myself. I had not started the tour well. For some reason I can't explain even now, my keeping went in the first match against the Young West Indies team in Pointe-a-Pierre. I know I missed one stumping and a catch I would normally have taken with ease and that worried me. Thanks to Ken Barrington and Geoff Miller who put me through a tough series of special work-outs in St Vincent, I felt I had got it all back together again by the time of the first one day international.

The wash-out of the four day match against Guyana was another huge disappointment. After missing that first Test I had been picked to play against Guyana and was looking forward again to getting back into action and making my bid to take over from Paul for the second Test. The wash out ruined that chance but I was pleased to keep my place for the one day international in Berbice.

The only way for us to travel was by air and even that meant a dawn rising to get there in time. First by a light aircraft to a small air strip just outside New Amsterdam — the main town in Berbice — and then the helicopter swoop which dumped us down on the outfield and within yards of the pavilion. We had been crammed in like sardines with bats, pads and other cricketing equipment stacked all around us so that there wasn't an inch to move. Our return journey was by helicopter all the way to an army base within a mile or so of our hotel where Geoff Boycott commandeered a jeep and had us swiftly back. We had tried to persuade the helicopter pilot to land us on the tennis courts next to the hotel but he wasn't having any of it.

The only other way to Berbice was by road which included a ferry crossing over the Berbice River. That would have been impossible. If everything had gone smoothly, it would have taken us three hours. And very little runs smoothly in Guyana, particularly on the roads where you have to compete with thirty year old cars, donkey carts, cows, pigs, goats and chickens which are allowed to roam freely even on the main highways. And there was no guarantee that the ferry would run on time as the many cricket fans who travelled up from Georgetown discovered and missed the start.

After the wash-out in Georgetown we were keen to get back to some cricket but we were not in the right frame of mind to tackle an international match. The Robin Jackman issue had broken the evening before, the tour was in a state of confusion and we woke up on the morning of the match still uncertain as to whether we would play. It was not the ideal preparation for such an important game.

In many ways, the trip to Berbice was worthwhile even for those not playing just to see the ground. In the circumstances manager Alan Smith had insisted on the whole party going to show a united front in the face of the political row. We had expected it to be a typical country ground, few stands, short of amenities and with large open spaces all around.

Instead we found one of the best grounds in the Caribbean with large, attractive double decker stands around two thirds of the ground, a flat and smooth outfield and a goodish wicket although it took spin throughout the day, and an enthusiastic crowd.

The ground holds about seventeen thousand when full and there must have been almost that number packed inside by the time we arrived forty-five minutes before the scheduled start. Naturally they wanted the West Indies to win but we all found them ready to applaud and salute us whenever we did anything to catch their eye. They knew their cricket too, as you might expect from an area which has produced such players as Rohan Kanhai and Alvin Kallicharran.

Perhaps the most impressive item on the ground — as we were to find on most Caribbean grounds — was the sight screens at each end. Ours in England are a low quality by comparison, even on our Test match grounds. Being behind the bowler's arm and in line with the wicket is always the best place to be on any ground if you want to know exactly what is happening, how the bowler is performing and what affect the wicket conditions is having on the ball. That is one reason why, in England, we have seats at each end of the ground behind the wickets even though they are a nuisance with people constantly moving and holding up play. There is no trouble of that sort in the West Indies with all their main grounds being equipped with large, concrete sightscreens covering the entire width of the square. The Queen's Park Oval, Port of Spain, Trinidad is the one exception. There one end is occupied by the main pavilion and has virtually no sightscreen. To be fair, it is easier to provide these large sightscreens in the West Indies where most squares have only two or perhaps three wickets. In England — especially on the major grounds — the square can have as many as 10 wickets and it would need giant sightscreens to protect all of them.

We had made one change in our one day side. Graham Dilley, who had missed the first international because of a stomach upset, returned in place of my Yorkshire colleague Chris Old. The West Indies side was much stronger than in the first game. They had lost Alvin Kallicharran because of a broken hand received in a domestic Shell Shield match but Gordon Greenidge and Viv Richards were back in action having recovered from injury and illness respectively. They fielded, in fact, the winning Test side which meant that they were still one genuine bowler short.

It meant that Clive Lloyd was forced to fiddle with Viv Richards and Larry Gomes to complete their fifty overs. Neither is regarded as a front line spinner. They are known in the trade as 'Mickey Mouse' bowlers and we knew we would have to get after them to build a decent score when Clive won the toss and asked us to bat first. We knew we were going to struggle to score heavily against the fast men.

As it turned out Gomes was almost the match winner and I have to give credit to Clive for the way he used his two part-time off spinners. He virtually rushed them into the attack as soon as Andy Roberts had given him his first breakthrough by having Graham Gooch caught behind getting a top edge hooking at a shortish delivery. It was a stroke Graham would never have played at that stage in a first class game but a justifiable risk in a one day game.

With only 16 runs on the board and seven overs gone, it meant that we were under pressure and Clive brought on Viv and Larry as a partnership. He realised we wanted to attack them yet we could not do so in a wholehearted way so early in the innings. They took the next four wickets between them to leave us on 62 for five with almost half our overs gone.

Viv made the first strike. Geoff Boycott made room to cut a long hop but was bowled when the ball never got up more than a couple of feet off the ground. Then it was Larry Gomes' turn with the next three wickets including Mike Gatting and Roland Butcher, two former colleagues of his during his days on the Middlesex staff.

David Gower was his first victim however. The wicket had been a little damp in the morning and encouraged spin as it dried. Larry made one bite and David was well beaten by the turn as he played a forward defensive stroke. Roland Butcher was caught at backward square leg attempting to sweep and Mike Gatting fell to a catch at mid-on after playing extremely well for his 29, the first time he had had a bat in his hands for twenty-one days.

With half the side out we were almost 20 runs worse off than we had been in our first one day international when bowled out for 125. We knew we faced a struggle to pass that modest total but just managed to creep beyond it.

Once again skipper Ian Botham played a major part in rebuilding our innings. Peter Willey proved a valuable ally in a 46 run sixth wicket partnership in 14 overs which ended just before lunch and took me to the wicket when Willey was bowled by Colin Croft. It was an awkward time to go in. The fast bowlers were coming back for their final fling and it also meant I had to start my innings twice. Lunch and tea intervals often prove a useful wicket taker when batsmen have to play themselves in again. So it proved in Berbice. Botham had added only one to his lunchtime total when he was out, dying an agonising death. He attempted to pull a short ball from Roberts. He missed it completely, the ball keeping a little lower than he expected, and could only watch in horror as it struck his thigh, trickled down his leg and fell on the wicket.

I soon lost my new partner John Emburey who was caught at mid-off, managed to add 13 for the ninth wicket with Graham Stevenson before being completely deceived by Colin Croft and the innings folded soon after with us bowled out for 137.

Modest as it was, it began to look even more insignificant when we were all back in the dressing room. Joel Garner had been the most expensive West Indies bowler and had failed to take a wicket. Yet he still managed to inflict a great deal of damage to our side. He had bowled a yorker to Graham Dilley which landed right on our fast bowler's big toe on his right foot — the foot he drags along the ground when he bowls.

The toe was a bit of a mess. Graham tried to bowl. In fact he managed four overs before going off for a little treatment because he was in so much pain. He returned for one more but it was hopeless and he was forced to leave the field. With only half his overs bowled, we had lost our main strike bowler.

Even so I felt that we might have won the match if one run out decision had gone our way. I had already claimed one run out victim in Gordon Greenidge and felt I was successful in running out Desmond Haynes as well before he had reached double figures. By then Viv Richards had been dismissed and the West Indies would have been 30 odd for three and under pressure. That's when they start panicking. Instead Haynes was given the benefit of the doubt and went on to be their top scorer.

The one run out decision that went my way almost didn't. Despite the toe injury, Graham Dilley was really steaming in and I was standing some fifteen yards back when he bowled to Gordon Greenidge. Gordon turned him to square leg and immediately he played the shot I heard him shout to Desmond Haynes 'one'. With Roland Butcher, a superb fielder, at mid-wicket, I knew it was going to be tight and I set off racing up to the wicket.

Roland's pick up right handed was smooth but his aim was a little awry as he attempted to throw down the wicket. I was racing in at full pelt and had to reach beyond the wicket to gather the ball. By the time I had pulled up I was a couple of yards down the pitch with Desmond bearing down at me. I knew I did not have time to run up to the wicket to take the bails off so hurled the ball instead. Fortunately it clipped the off stump with Desmond still a yard out of his ground.

That wicket fell in Dilley's second over. In his third he got rid of Viv Richards who pulled at a short pitched delivery only to get a top edge and send it many a mile in the air. At first it looked as though it might even go for six but the ball started to drop just inside the boundary edge at long leg and Graham Stevenson took a well judged catch. He would have had time to take out a cigarette and light it waiting for the ball to come down. Those catches are never easy.

At that stage the West Indies were 11 for two and only five more had been added when I thought I had run out Haynes. New batsman Everton Mattis steered a delivery from Botham down to the third man boundary where John Emburey fielded the ball cleanly and sent it back to be right over the wicket. It was a superb throw and all I had to do was take off the bails as Haynes realised the danger and made a desperate full length dive for the crease. I shall forever remain convinced that the run out was clean but the square leg umpire had no hesitation in shaking his head.

The West Indies had 90 on the board before Haynes made his next mistake and was caught at deep square leg attempting to whip John Emburey off his toes. By then he had lost his partner Mattis in another strange incident.

I didn't like the suggestion that Mattis was making when he stood in his crease shouting 'No man, no' when we all appealed for his dismissal after he had been bowled by John Emburey. He played forward to a ball which pitched middle and leg and took his leg stump having touched his left leg on the way through. John and I immediately appealed when the bail came off but Mattis just stood his ground saying 'No man, no' over and over again which could only mean that he thought I must have knocked the bail off with pads or hands as I gathered the ball. I didn't like that implication.

While Mattis just stood there refusing to go, the umpire at the bowler's end — Compton Vyfhuis — made no move to give him out. John and I appealed again. Ian Botham joined in this time racing up to the middle of the wicket and it was only when Vyfhuis spoke to his square leg colleague that he made his decision. I'm not quite sure how he thought the wicket had been broken if it had not been done by John's bowling but Desmond Haynes confirmed that from his view from the non striker's end, Mattis had been bowled cleanly enough.

The wickets of Mattis and Haynes were the only others we were to get as Clive Lloyd joined Larry Gomes and took the West Indies to victory with 10.3 overs to spare. It was another great disappointment for us. I don't like losing even a practice match but our defeat on this occasion was understandable and predictable after all that we had been through.

You can't go for an entire week not playing cricket and expect to get the better of a team as powerful as this present West Indies side. Especially one that had been in constant practice with six of their side having played in a Shell Shield match in Barbados while we had been sampling the strength of the South American rain. The worst was still to come for it was on our arrival back in our Georgetown Hotel that

One day international in St Vincent.

Peter Willey batting in the St Vincent one day international.

Graham Gooch hits a four against Trinidad and Tobago and (below) *Geoff Boycott batting in the same match.*

An all too frequent sight during the tour.

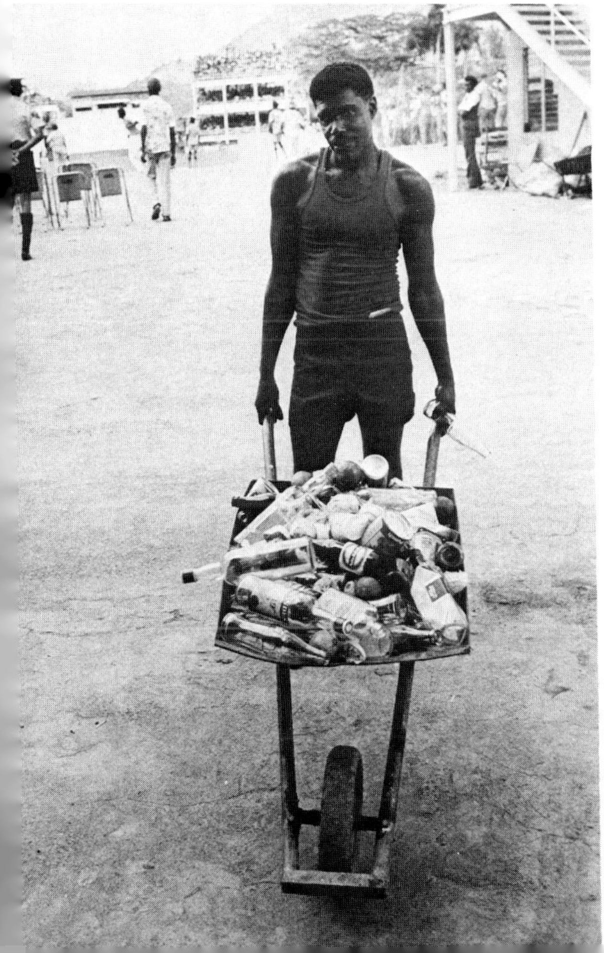

Bottles collected from the pitch in Trinidad following the trouble due to the late start of the first Test.

Paul Downton in his first Test appearance for England; Trinidad, first Test.

John Emburey bowling during the first Test.

Three faces of Robin Jackman; (top left) *being served with the deportation order in Georgetown;* (left) *in a relaxed mood before the third Test in Barbados and* (above) *in a reflective mood during the third Test which was his first Test appearance for England.*

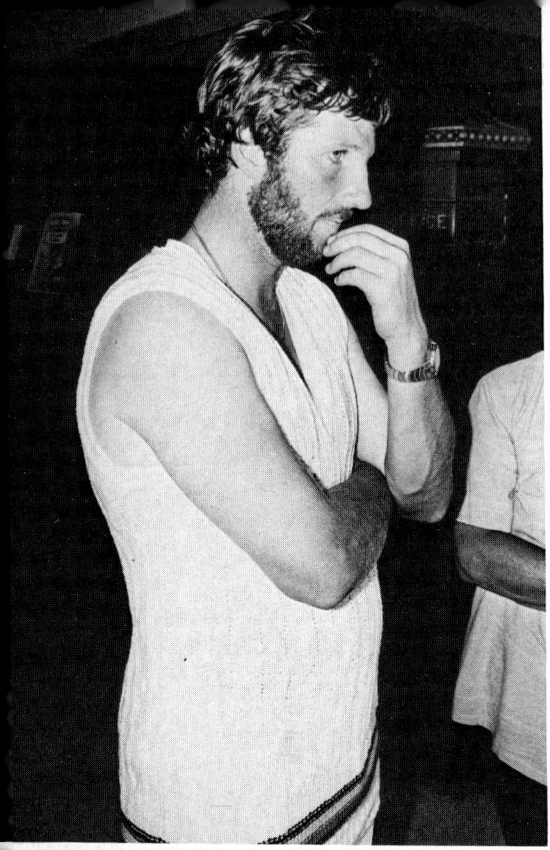

(left) *A worried Ian Botham waits in the hotel foyer whilst Robin Jackman is served with the deportation order.*

(below) *England manager Alan Smith (centre) and Philip Mallet (right), British High Commissioner, at the press conference in Georgetown when it was announced that the England team would leave Guyana.*

Softball cricket in Barbados.

Bernard Thomas, England physiotherapist, doing back exercises with England keeper David Bairstow.

(top) *A dejected England team during the two minutes silence which was paid in memory of Ken Barrington.*

(above) *Roland Butcher makes his first England Test appearance in his native Barbados in the third Test.*

The West Indies captain, Clive Lloyd, on his way to a century in the first innings of the third Test.

Michael Holding bowls John Emburey a bouncer during the third Test.

Graham Dilley bowling in the third Test.

Ian Botham hits out; Barbados, third Test.

(top left) *David Gower bowled by Viv Richards in the third Test.*

(bottom left) *Graham Gooch is clean bowled by Holding in the third Test.*

(above) *The greatest fast bowling combination ever: (left to right) Andy Roberts, Michael Holding, Colin Croft, Joel Garner.*

(left) *Viv Richards batting during his 180 not out in the third* Test.

(below) *Jubilant West Indies fans after their victory in the third Test.*

manager Alan Smith called us together in Ian Botham's room and told us that deportation orders were about to be served on Robin Jackman. We knew then that the Guyana leg was over. Another six days were to go by before we were to discover whether the rest of the tour was to continue.

WEST INDIES *v*. ENGLAND (one day international)

England		
G. Boycott	b Richards	7
G. A. Gooch	c Murray b Roberts	11
M. W. Gatting	c Mattis b Gomes	29
D. I. Gower	b Gomes	3
R. O. Butcher	c Haynes b Gomes	5
*I. T. Botham	b Roberts	27
P. Willey	b Croft	21
+D. L. Bairstow	b Croft	16
J. E. Emburey	c Croft b Holding	0
G. B. Stevenson	not out	8
G. R. Dilley	b Croft	3
Extras	b 4, lb 2, nb 1	7
Total	47.2 overs	137

Fall of Wickets: 1—16, 2—27, 3—34, 4—59, 5—62, 6—108, 7—112, 8—119, 9—132

Bowling: Roberts 7—0—17.2; Holding 7—1—13—1; Richards 10—0—26—1; Croft 6.2—1—9—3; Gomes 10—2—30—3; Garner 7—2—35—0.

West Indies		
C. G. Greenidge	run out	2
D. L. Haynes	c Gooch b Emburey	48
I. V. A. Richards	c Stevenson b Dilley	3
E. Mattis	b Emburey	24
H. A. Gomes	not out	22
*C. H. Lloyd	not out	25
Extras	b 4, lb 8, nb 2	14
Total	(4 wkts) 39.3 overs	138

+D. A. Murray, A. M. E. Roberts, M. E. Holding, J. Garner, C. E. H. Croft did not bat

Fall of wickets: 1—6, 2—11, 3—85, 4—90

Bowling: Dilley 5—0—21—1; Botham 7—1—24—0; Stevenson 6—0—21—0; Emburey 10—4—22—2; Gooch 2—0—8—0; Willey 9—0—23—0; Gower 0.3—0—5—0

* captain + wicket-keeper

West Indies won by 6 wickets

9 ROBIN JACKMAN (SURREY & ENGLAND) & ALAN SMITH (ENGLAND MANAGER)

The background to what had become known as the 'Jackman Affair' is told here by the two people most involved.

My wife Yvonne was on the other end of the telephone call which woke me up in my hotel room in Bridgetown, Barbados and ended my ten days of personal and private agony. Not only my agony but hers as well which was why it was so appropriate that she should be the first to tell me that England's tour of the West Indies was to continue with me as a full member of the party.

As thoughtful as ever, she had waited until midday in England before phoning me at eight in the morning Barbados time so as not to disturb my night's sleep. She assumed I would have known by then. 'You have heard the news?' she asked. 'No' I replied. 'The tour is still on' she almost shrieked down the telephone.

I could understand her feeling of joy. My deportation from Georgetown, Guyana and the resulting cancellation of the second Test will go down in cricket history, I suppose, as the 'Jackman Affair of 1981'. In truth I must confess I knew very little of what was happening at the time, so skilfully did manager Alan Smith shield me from the media and hassle. I simply knew that my name was making news. Yvonne at home felt the whole exposure — and suffered as a result.

She was born in South Africa. On the few occasions I managed to get through to her, I had to assure her that she was nothing to do with the issue and had never been involved. Just in the same way the manager and the rest of the England team constantly re-assured me during our desperate hours together in Georgetown that I was not to blame myself in any way. I was grateful for their support although, as I said earlier, I did not realise then that my name was sending shudders throughout the cricketing world just as the name of Basil D'Oliveira had done twelve years before when England's tour of South Africa was called off in 1968 because the country of his birth refused to accept 'Dolly' as a member of England's touring side.

Throughout his troubles Basil refused to become involved in any political issues saying repeatedly that he was a cricketer who was willing to play against anybody at anytime. I felt exactly the same way in Guyana and still do today. It was not until Alan Smith agreed to help me put the record straight in this chapter that I learned for the first time what exactly had happened.

Yet when the buzz first started in Georgetown that enquiries were being made about my South African connections as the Guyanese Government put it, I couldn't help thinking of the irony of the situation. The only reason I had gone to South Africa in the first place back in 1968 was to make myself into a better bowler for Surrey in the hope that I would also catch the eye of the England selectors.

Ever since that time I had been hoping that I would one day get a chance to represent my country in a Test match. Several times in the past I thought I had been near. I had been picked to play in one day internationals but missed out when it came to Test cricket. Last summer at home, my best in England when taking 121 wickets, I had also played for England in a one day international against Australia but missed out again when left out of the team for the Centenary Test at Lord's and selection for the winter tour of the Caribbean.

At the age of thirty-five I thought my last chance had gone when I failed to make the touring party. Then came the injury to Bob Willis followed by a phone call to my home late one night from Donald Carr, secretary of the Test and County Cricket Board. As soon as he mentioned my name, I knew I was the one chosen to be sent out to the West Indies as Bob's replacement. He did not have to say any more.

This was the moment I had been waiting for. The moment my winters in southern Africa playing for Western Province and then Rhodesia — now Zimbabwe — in the Currie Cup and making myself a better bowler on their harder wickets, had proved to be worthwhile.

A moment, incidentally, I do not think I would have achieved without the help of West Indies and Barbados pace bowler Sylvester Clarke. Playing for Surrey in 1980 he proved so difficult to score against with the new ball that I am sure many county batsmen took extra risks against me which helped me to my best ever season.

I could not have felt better when I stepped off the plane in Georgetown, Guyana, even though I was tired after the flight from London and it was the middle of the night. I don't think I could have felt more miserable the following Thursday — only four days later — when a Guyanese immigration official approached me and said 'I hereby serve you . . . ' I don't recall the rest of the words he used. It was strictly legal jargon as the official played everything by the book. But I do recall his final words when he said 'We would like you to leave the country as quickly as possible'.

Even though the manager had warned me what was going to happen when I was called to his room to have my visa cancelled in my passport, I was still staggered. I did not think I had done anything wrong in going to South Africa to earn a living in the winter as a professional cricketer. Not only earn a living helping Rhodesia but coaching black as well as white schoolchildren so that they could grow up together and hopefully play the game at a senior level side by side without any hassle and bad feeling just as we do every day of the week in our domestic cricket. A scene where white South Africans play alongside and against West Indians without bickering over coloured issues and enjoy the company of each other to the full.

Only two hours before I was served with the deportation order I was even wondering whether I might have made my Test debut in Georgetown within less than a week of arriving in the country and joining the tour party. I would not have been fully acclimatised, probably not fully fit although I had kept myself in shape back at home as one of the standby fast bowlers in case of injury. But suddenly that possibility of a Test debut had been taking shape largely because there was nobody else available to complete the England pace attack.

On the Tuesday before the Test was due to start on Saturday 28 February, Chris Old had damaged his left shoulder bowling in a practice match. He had flown with the rest of the party to Berbice for the one day international the following day with his arm in a sling and was clearly an unlikely starter for the second Test. Then, during the game in Berbice, Graham Dilley was hit on the toe by Joel Garner whilst batting, an injury that was to put him out of cricket for a week.

It was on the helicopter ride back to our hotel from Berbice that it suddenly struck me what those injuries meant. They left only the captain Ian Botham, Graham Stevenson and myself to complete the three man England pace attack. I wasn't ready. On the journey out from England I had studied the tour intinerary and thought the earliest I would play would be in Montserrat after the third Test. But I was prepared to have a go.

At that stage I knew little of the trouble ahead. Two days earlier the manager had called me aside and asked me for details of my last trip to South Africa in the winter of 1979–80. The day before he had told me not to worry but had warned me that senior Government ministers were now involved in the situation and that I was not to say a word to anybody. As far as I was concerned at the time, there was no serious question of the second Test match being called off because I was an unacceptable member of the touring party.

I knew the worst however as soon as I arrived back to our Georgetown hotel following the one day international defeat. Everybody who owned a camera in Georgetown seemed to be crowded into the hotel lobby along with cricket writers, other journalists I did not recognise and the television cameras as I was hustled through and up to the captain's room along with the rest of the players and told to stay there. Our manager had told me not to worry but to get on with my cricket and the problem of getting Test match fit as soon as possible. I hadn't worried. My cricket had been my only concern. Only now in writing this have I learned of exactly what went on, the fears and frustrations of the manager and it is best that he should explain them. Over to you Alan.

Robin had been in Georgetown almost forty hours having passed through immigration on arrival at Timehri Airport without the slightest delay or question mark when I was given the first hint that there could be trouble over his presence in Guyana. A little ironically that indication was given to me whilst I was enjoying the hospitality of the Police Commissioner and a number of his deputies in their Mess alongside the cricket field on the Guyana Police Sports Ground.

They had looked after us very well, offering us every facility and worked hard to accommodate us when we asked permission to use their ground following the heavy rain which had made play impossible on the Bourda Test ground in Georgetown. We had been invited to a reception that Tuesday evening by former Glamorgan and West Indies opening batsman Comrade Roy Fredericks who was Minister of State for Youth and Sports in Guyana. It left very little time to spare between the end of the practice session and the start of the reception but I agreed to go to the Mess to meet the Police Commissioner and half a dozen Deputy Commissioners to be able to say thank you for their assistance.

I was just enjoying a friendly drink when Roy Fredericks arrived at the Mess with another former West Indies batsman Joe Solomon who is now President of the Guyana Cricket Association. They asked me if they could have a quiet word. Joe told me, 'We have something of a problem. A number of people are becoming anxious about the circumstances of Jackman's last visit to South Africa and could you give me the details.' I told him I had little idea of the circumstances but I would certainly find out. It was at that stage that I first became alerted and had every right to be when Joe added 'The Government may take a serious view over it' to which I replied, 'You had better see to it that they don't because the consequences may be far reaching.'

At that early stage I sensed what the Guyana Government involvement could mean and I also knew what our stand would be although I would have to have it confirmed by Lord's. I knew we would not agree to any interference with the selection of our side.

That brief conversation with Joe Solomon was enough for me to call the British High Commissioner in Guyana, Mr Philip Mallet, immediately I returned to our hotel and asked to see him. Fortunately his house was near to the hotel and I called in on the way to the reception and reported what I had been told. At first he did not think there was any need to worry but half way through the reception — after he had had a chance to make his own enquiries — he drew me to one side and told me 'I'm inclined to think they may make more of this than I first thought'.

I had no wish to alarm Robin. At that stage I just told him I had been asked about his last visit to South Africa during the winter of 1979/80 and to give me a brief run down. He told me he had been in Rhodesia — now Zimbabwe — and had played for them in the Currie Cup as well as doing some coaching, mostly of white children but with some coloured children as well.

The following day, whilst the players were having their own practice match between themselves back on the police ground, it became even more clear that the Guyana Government was going to take a tough line. At the same time I took every opportunity to stress our position to both Roy Fredericks and Robin Corbin, the Minister for National Development who was becoming a regular caller. I told them that if Guyana did not let us select our team freely, they must be prepared for the consequences that we could not play. 'We have sixteen players here from which to pick our side for the Test match and we will pick freely from those sixteen.'

Robin was not involved personally at that stage. I did not want him to be. Even when Corbin and Fredericks visited me in the team's hotel late on the Wednesday evening and told me that the situation had passed out of their hands and was being dealt with by more senior Ministers, I did not feel Robin should be worried although the Government had, by then, issued a formal statement saying they were investigating his connections with South Africa.

His job was to play cricket. The following day, Thursday 26 February, we were playing the second one day international against the West Indies in Berbice which meant a dawn start. Although Robin wasn't playing because it was too soon after his arrival from England, I wanted him to go to Berbice without any thoughts clouding his mind. It was essential that he should quickly become acclimatised to the conditions without having anything extra to worry about.

By that Wednesday evening it became clear to me that I

could not afford to go to Berbice. In addition to what will now go down in cricket history as the 'Jackman Affair' I was also involved in seeing Brian Rose off back to England following the discovery that he had a slight defect in his right eye. I wanted to see him off at the airport but was denied that opportunity.

I called on Mr Mallet again and it became quite clear early in the morning that Robin's entry visa could be cancelled. That immediately posed an additional problem as far as I was concerned — the personal safety of the players. Over the years a succession of touring sides have encountered crowd problems in Georgetown. Now they were going to be denied a Test match several thousand Guyanese had been looking forward to for some months, saving to pay for their tickets. With the media Government controlled, I was a little fearful how the facts were to be presented to the Guyanese public and whether the public might take their annoyance out on us.

I asked Mr Mallet if he could arrange for additional security and police protection for the team's hotel. In addition I started investigating ways of getting the team away from Georgetown as quickly as possible. I was determined that we would all leave together — certainly the nineteen strong England party and the thirty or so journalists and television representatives who were following us. If there was not sufficient room on any scheduled flight I asked the High Commission to investigate the chances of chartering an aircraft.

Throughout the developments I had kept Donald Carr, Secretary of the Test and County Cricket Board, fully informed at Lord's but with no fresh news at lunchtime, I returned to the hotel to finalise Brian Rose's departure. It proved to be the lull before the storm.

Earlier in the day Mr Mallet had made our position perfectly clear when he told a press conference that Robin's arrival had not broken the terms of the 1977 Gleneagles Agreement as far as the British Government was concerned. He added, 'Surely Jackman is here as a member of a multi-racial side to play a multi-racial West Indian team in multi-racial Guyana.'

Meanwhile I was back in my hotel room, attempting to listen to the radio to discover how the England team was faring in Berbice. My listening was interrupted at 4.10 in the afternoon when I received a phone call from Mr Gordon Johnstone, the second secretary in the High Commission asking me to go to see the High Commissioner as soon as possible. Within ten minutes Mr Mallet was telling me that the Guyanese Government had decided that Robin was not a permitted immigrant and would be served with an order to leave the country.

For the next two hours I spoke with Donald Carr and read over to him the statement that was to be issued by Comrade Rashleigh Jackson, Guyana's Foreign Minister. It was taken down in shorthand and the Cricket Council's statement was prepared in answer.

By the time I returned to the hotel, the team had just started to arrive back from Berbice. Robin knew immediately that something was in the air. The hotel lobby was filled with newspapermen, photographers and television reporters, the news having leaked that Robin was to be deported. I had warned every member of the team twenty-four hours earlier that they must not make any public statement and asked Ian to take them all to his room and keep them there while Mr Mallet and I held a press conference.

We read out the following statement from Comrade Jackson:

'Following an investigation, the Guyana Government is satisfied that Robin Jackman, the English cricketer now in Guyana, has played in South Africa recently and subsequent to the adoption of the Gleneagles Accord.

'The Gleneagles Accord was reached in Scotland in 1977 during a break in the Commonwealth Heads of Government Conference in London. In effect that Accord denounces apartheid in sports and frowns on sporting contacts with South Africa by Commonwealth countries.

'In the Accord the member countries of the Commonwealth acknowledge that the full realisation of their objectives involved the understanding, separate and active participation of the nationals of their country and of their national sports organisations and authorities.

'The Heads of Government at that time also specifically welcomed the belief expressed at their meeting that in the light of their consultation and accord, there were unlikely to be future sporting contacts of any significance between Commonwealth countries or their nationals and South Africa while that country continues to pursue their detestable policy of apartheid.

'The Guyana Government has strong and well publicised views against apartheid in sports and has in the past taken appropriate action against persons who come or wished to come to Guyana hoping to participate in sports after doing so in South Africa.

'Following the confirmation that Jackman has recently played cricket in South Africa, the Minister of Foreign Affairs, Cde R. E. Jackson, received and discusssed the matter with the British High Commissioner to Guyana, Mr Philip Mallet on Wednesday, 25 February at 16.15 hours.

'The Guyana Government knows that although attention has been drawn to the fact that the cricketer's action is not in accordance with the spirit and letter of the Gleneagles Accord, he has neither withdrawn from the team nor has he left Guyana.

'In the light of the above circumstances the Guyana Government has been constrained to issue today an order revoking the two week visitors permit which was given to Robin Jackman on arrival.'

We also read out the following statement from the Cricket Council:

'The Guyanese Minister of Foreign Affairs has informed the British High Commissioner that Mr Jackman's permission to stay in Guyana is being revoked.

'The Cricket Council has informed the Manager of the England Touring Team that as Robin Jackman has been asked to leave Guyana it is no longer possible for the Test team to be chosen without restrictions being imposed. It is therefore with deep regret that England cannot take part in the second Test due to start on Saturday.

'The Cricket Council does not consider that the inclusion of Robin Jackman in the England touring team in any way infringes the spirit or letter of the Gleneagles Agreement.

'The Council will be seeking immediate assurances from the West Indies Cricket Board that there will be absolutely no attempt by any government to interfere with the selection of the England team or to impose any restrictions on their entry to any country included on the itinerary for the remainder of the tour.'

At this stage the players themselves did not know what was happening. I went up to Ian's room and told them simply. 'There will be no Test match in Guyana on Saturday. We have got to leave here as quickly as possible.'

We were still all gathered there when I was told that two men had arrived at the hotel to see Robin. I made arrangements to see them in the room of the hotel manager. One was in uniform and the other in plain clothes. I told them I would take them to my room where they could see Robin. They handed a piece of paper to Robin and asked for his passport. The visa was revoked and dated and he was given another piece of paper saying that he was no longer a permitted immigrant. They told me that Robin was to leave as quickly as possible but I told them that there was no way Robin was leaving by himself. I said that we would all leave as a group and it was up to the Government to help us. I suppose it would have been within their rights to have removed Robin forcibly and I was prepared to create a scene if they had attempted to do so.

Once the deportation order had been served, my immediate concern was the safety of the players. With the media being controlled by the Government, I was a little concerned as to how they would present the news that the Test match had been cancelled. Once again the local police co-operated efficiently. The outside security guard on the hotel was more than doubled with uniformed men and a number of plain clothes police mingled with the visitors to the hotel.

Once that had been arranged, my next target was to make sure that we got out of Georgetown the following day. The longer we stayed, the greater the danger that the Government would take some action to force Robin out ahead of the rest of us. I was not going to let that happen and was willing to try any other method of leaving the country if the scheduled air flights were full. There was not an aircraft available for us to charter. I asked if it were possible for the Army to supply a coach and we could drive out through the jungle and swamps to reach the Surinam border. That was possible.

Crossing into Surinam was not. The two countries are divided by a river four miles wide. Our exit that way was blocked. My next line of approach also drew a blank. I made enquiries to see whether the British Government had a destroyer or some other naval craft in the area which could have been diverted to Georgetown to evacuate us. Earlier in the tour we had come across HMS *Intrepid* which was making a courtesy call on some of the Caribbean Islands and it was possible there might have been another craft somewhere in the local waters but there was not one available to have reached Guyana in time. The only way out of Georgetown was by air. Some strings were pulled somewhere for on the Friday morning I was told that twenty-three seats were suddenly made available for us. I can only guess that there were some disappointed travellers that day who found their bookings cancelled at the last moment.

At least the team could get out but I also felt concern for the journalists travelling with us. Again some strings were pulled and forty-five minutes before we were due to leave the hotel I was told that British West Indies Airways had substituted a Boeing 707 for the scheduled DC 9 and there would be room for everybody.

My other concern was that Robin should not feel at all guilty for what had happened. I stressed to him, 'You must not feel that any part of this is your fault. You must not feel in any way to blame. As far as the team, the Test and County Cricket Board and the Cricket Council are concerned you have been properly picked to come on this tour and you must view everything in that light.' I must confess that I was very relieved once the 707 left the runway of Timehri Airport some two hours behind schedule because of the need to find another crew for the aircraft.

Arriving in Barbados seemed like heaven. The mood of everybody brightened with the friendly greeting at the airport although the situation was extremely delicate. We sensed that everybody wanted us to play but the Foreign Ministers of Barbados and Antigua plus the Deputy Chief Minister of the British Crown Colony of Montserrat and a senior civil servant from Jamaica were meeting over the weekend to decide whether they agreed with Guyana's interpretation of the Gleneagles Agreement or whether we would be welcomed everywhere on the rest of the scheduled tour with Robin a member of the team.

We had to act as though the tour was going ahead planning a week of cricket so that the players would be ready to continue where they left off if and when they were given the nod. Yet everything had to be done in such a way that it could not be interpreted as over confidence on our part and seen as an attempt to put pressure on the governments involved. I was very conscious that one indiscreet word might wreck everything we were attempting to do to serve cricket in the broadest sense. Nobody was allowed to be interviewed even in my presence, and nobody has even now.

There was one other vitally important consideration — the financial one which struck me immediately probably because of my role as a cricket administrator back home. Whilst waiting to get out of Guyana it struck me that if the tour was to be aborted there would be a heavy financial loss for the West Indies Board of Control and the local cricket associations some of whom had spent considerable amounts of money improving their grounds for our visit. In addition the Test and County Cricket Board would suffer having to meet a handsome slice of the tour expenses themselves including travelling and wages which, in turn, would effect the income each county organisation in England receives from the TCCB. It seemed to me that in the general short term interests of the game as a whole we had to adopt a positive attitude to keep the tour going never mind the long term. If the tour had been aborted then what the consequences would have been I dread to think. As it happened the tour guarantee to the TCCB was not altered in any way despite the loss of the second Test with the crowds at the last three Tests exceptionally good.

At the start of the discussion Peter Short, President of the Barbados Cricket Association and a former secretary of the West Indies Cricket Board, and I were fairly confident that the tour would go ahead as scheduled from all the indications we had. Our mood began to change as the talks took up the best part of three days.

They had started on the Sunday following our arrival on Friday 27 February. On the Tuesday we were told that the verdict was likely to be announced around 2 pm. An hour before then I was lodged in my hotel room with Peter keeping me company while the team were playing in a practice match among themselves. Later we heard that there had been a hitch with one of the Governments involved — possibly Jamaica — and that the verdict would probably not be announced until the Wednesday morning.

It was — in the early hours long after Peter had gone home and the England players and myself had gone to bed. Yet another night's sleep interrupted when I had a call from an English journalist soon after midnight to say the Press were to be given the verdict at one in the morning and would I be available for comment almost immediately afterwards.

I had very little sleep that night. But this was one occasion I didn't mind. The Ministers had been tracked down by a few English cricket writers to their hideaway in Barbados and the verdict the cricket world had been waiting for was handed out to them on the doorstep of their hotel room. Along with a copy to Peter Short who had been summoned to the hotel. I had just time to hear the news that the tour was to continue without any conditions, read the statement quickly before I was involved in press, radio and television interviews long into the night.

I saw little point in waking the players then and telling them. That is why Mrs Jackman just beat me to it the following morning as I started to ring round the rooms of the players to inform them. Their relief was obvious, just as mine had been six and half hours earlier. Back to Robin.

It was not until I had been in Barbados for a couple of days that I first realised just how big the story of my deportation had been and the full significance of it struck me. I knew my name had passed from the sports pages to the news pages. I had seen that happen in Georgetown. On the morning we left Guyana, the whole front page of the morning newspaper had been devoted to my deportation and the decision of the Cricket Council to call off the second Test as a result. It had all been reported in a straight, matter-of-fact way without any interpretation or comment at that stage.

My story was front page again when I arrived in Barbados

where the newspapers have the freedom to comment. Most were in favour of the tour continuing although some politicians saw an opportunity to create extra publicity for themselves by denouncing my presence. But it was only when I saw copies of the English newspapers – copies a few days old – that I realised it had been the lead story and my name must have been dominating the headlines. My wife Yvonne had been besieged by newspapermen and photographers at our Surrey home to such an extent that I was forced to demand that she went away to give her some rest.

I had no idea until I phoned her from Barbados just how much she had been involved. I had not been able to get through from Georgetown on the evening I had been given my 'marching orders'. That evening and the following morning when we made our flight to freedom, the telephones had all been commandeered by the cricket writers although I managed to get a message to her through Donald Carr at Lord's asking her not to worry.

It was only when I read the English newspapers that I realised the danger facing the whole future of cricket if the other Caribbean Governments had followed the same line as Guyana. That I could be responsible for the break up of cricket as we know it now and the formation of two separate cricket circuits, one all white involving Tests between New Zealand, England, South Africa and Austrailia and the other limited to India, Pakistan, West Indies and Sri Lanka.

Even when Barbados, Jamaica, Antigua and Montserrat agreed that the tour should continue without any interruptions or special conditions, the rumblings of my arrival in the Caribbean are not over. In the statement from the Governments accepting my presence it was emphasised that the whole question of individuals like myself who have had some sporting contact with South Africa would be raised again in the forthcoming Commonwealth Heads of Government meeting in Australia. It seems the 'Jackman Affair' is not over yet.

I didn't realise the implications of my case largely because of the protection offered me by my manager and I am extremely grateful. He served me and the team magnificently throughout the whole episode, taking all the pressure, having sleepless nights while we concentrated as much as we could on our cricket and rest. The rest of the lads were magnificent as well. There was the usual mickey taking, even the suggestion of a thank you from many of them for my being responsible for getting them out of Guyana a week early. It is not a country which is high on the list of favourite places cricketers like to visit although the people we met couldn't do enough for us and many of them saw us off with tears in their eyes. They were shattered by the deportation order.

I can truthfully say that not once was I shown any animosity by anybody. There was one remark addressed to me when I played in my first match of the tour against Barbados. Over the years you learn to shut your ears to taunts from the crowd and I've no idea what the message was this time except that I heard the words 'South Africa' mentioned. That was the only time.

The great lengths the manager and the team went to protect me obviously helped me settle down quickly when we started playing cricket again. I was a spectator for the hastily arranged one day game against Barbados but found my rhythm surprisingly quickly when I played against Barbados in the four day game, finishing with four for 68 in their innings of 334, a performance which gave me my first Test cap.

The moment I had striven for over twenty years had finally arrived. And, after all that had gone on during the fortnight before, it was undoubtedly appropriate that I should walk into Test cricket for the first time alongside Roland Butcher — black and white together making their first Test appearances. I had not expected to play. Graham Dilley had recovered from his foot injury and filled the place I might have taken if the Guyana Test had been allowed to proceed. Chris Old had also recovered from his shoulder injury and Graham Stevenson was ahead of me as far as I was concerned.

I must have sealed my place with those four wickets against Barbados even though I used the old ball. I was grateful that the wicket in Barbados also has a little grass on it which helps me. But mostly I concentrated on my line and length and used all the experience I had gained for Surrey and Rhodesia to make sure I did not give any loose runs away.

I was determined that the batsmen would have to earn everything they took off me.

The grass on the Barbados wicket was a surprise to us all. Geoff Boycott, making his third tour of the Caribbean, confessed he had never seen one like it before. As I said, I was relieved. I had not really known what to expect when I flew in and I feared the worst when I saw my first West Indian wicket in Berbice.

As we flew over the ground in our helicopter my first impression was that the square was being protected by a brown cover despite the brilliant sunshine. When we landed I discovered the brown area was the square itself, a wide stretch of rolled mud. I was so surprised to find a blade of grass on it that I took a picture. Unfortunately it did not come out; just one more thing that went wrong in Guyana which is one country I shall never forget.

10 BILL ATHEY (YORKSHIRE & ENGLAND)

Bill Athey flies in from Australia to join the team in Barbados as a replacement for Brian Rose and tells of the disappointment he felt about his performance in the fourth Test.

The voice on the other end of the telephone put an end to my week of worrying. It belonged to Donald Carr, secretary of the Test and County Cricket Board phoning from Lord's. The message was fairly brief and simple. 'We want you to get to Barbados as quickly as possible. You could be playing on Saturday,' he said. There was only one slight problem. I was living in a Sydney suburb in Australia at the time.

That was my introduction to the tour of the West Indies in March, called in as a replacement for Brian Rose after it had been discovered he had an eye defect in Guyana. It's the second time I've stood in for Brian and gained an England cap as a result. I must buy him a drink when I next see him.

The only disadvantage about the phone call was that it came on a Wednesday which left me only forty-eight hours to get to Barbados in time to be considered for selection for the four day match against the island immediately before the third Test. In view of the urgency I was asked to make my own travel arrangements locally. Despite that, I made it in time before the team had been named to play Barbados — only to discover a couple of hours later that I had been ruled out because of my long journey.

I felt ready to play and was perfectly willing to play but being left on the sidelines in that match was a minor disappointment to the one I felt when left out of the touring party in the first place. That was the reason I found myself playing grade cricket in Sydney in an attempt to keep in trim during the English weather.

I thought I had a good chance of making his final 16 after scoring 32 and 51 for England in the two one day internationals against Australia towards the back end of the 1980 summer at home. I followed those with innings of 9 and 1 in the Cornhill Centenary Test. They were nothing to write home about but I had stayed around each time. I got those chances incidentally after Brian Rose, England's regular number three last summer against the West Indies, had been injured in the final Test against them.

For the four previous winters I had taken myself off to Australia during the break in the home season to play for Manly in their grade cricket. During the 1980 summer I had an offer to play for another Sydney grade side Balmain, an offer I put off accepting in the hope that I might be touring the West Indies instead.

As soon as I heard I wasn't in the touring squad although asked to keep in shape as one of the possible batting replacements, I contacted Balmain and told them I would be going to Australia if they still wanted me. Thankfully they did. At least it helped me to keep in some sort of touch with the bat even though Balmain went through a poorish time while I was there having several of their matches interrupted by rain.

My hopes of joining the rest of the England team were first raised by English newspapermen who rang me up and asked if I had heard anything officially from Lord's about dashing out as Brian's replacement. I had not. From then on I spent a rather anxious week waiting for news while the politicians in the West Indies were deciding whether the tour should continue after Robin Jackman's arrival and subsequent deportation from Guyana. The news of Jackman's troubles had broken about the same time as the cricket writers on the tour had been given a strong hint that I was the one the tour selectors had asked for immediately it had been decided that Brian should return home.

The phone call from Donald Carr put an end to all that speculation once it was learned the tour was to go ahead. And the start of a hectic three days for me. All I had been told was to get to Barbados and ask the New South Wales Cricket Association to pay the air fare for me and send on the bill to Lord's. Fortunately for me Quantas, the Australian airline, were a great help. Within an hour of getting in touch and explaining my position, they were back with all the bookings made on the first available flights. I didn't bother the NSW Cricket Association with the bill. I was staying in

Sydney at the home of another Balmain player Mark Byers and his father Fred happily settled the account saying he would reclaim it from Lord's later. I hope he has remembered.

It turned out to be quite a trip to keep the date with England in Bridgetown. I stopped at Pago-Pago, Honolulu and San Francisco when I changed planes. From there I went to New York where I changed planes again before finally arriving less than twenty-four hours before the scheduled start of the match against Barbados — only to learn I had not been considered because of my twenty-four hour journey. The dash had been for nothing although I felt good. After the hot, sticky weather in Sydney, adapting to the West Indian conditions was never going to be a problem. Although I felt a little tired the only place where I wanted to get my head down was out in the middle with a bat in my hand.

The fact that I was rather desperate to get a bat in my hands surprised everybody. Manager Alan Smith had been told that I was in good nick in Australia and had been getting runs after regular visits to the crease with Balmain. If I had not exactly set Sydney alight, at least I was supposed to be in better shape than anybody on the England tour after their rain hit start to the schedule. In fact I had played less cricket over the six weeks before my arrival in Barbados than the England team. I had been to the wicket only twice since the start of the year because of constant rain at the weekends. I was desperately short of practice.

That was one of the reasons why I was disappointed not to be playing in Barbados. I had also been looking forward to batting in better conditions than I had in Sydney. Grade cricket in Australia has a reputation for being fairly high class. In my experience it is and would be better if the wickets were improved. The grounds are owned by local councils which means that the wickets are maintained by them and not supervised by proper groundsmen as we know them in England.

In the main the wicket conditions are not top class and it was a great treat to find fairly decent wicket conditions under my feet when I did start batting in the West Indies. The England players told me that their practice facilities had been poor and it is essential to have decent nets playing against a side like the West Indies. They were very concerned about it considering the lengths to which county clubs go to providing the best for touring sides in England. But, decent or not, they had at least been getting net practice. I had not even had that in Australia.

There was another disappointment waiting for me when I did start playing — my own lack of form during the fourth Test in Antigua when dismissed for single figures in both innings of the drawn game.

It was strange because I had felt quite confident and satisfied with my two innings against the Leeward Islands in Montserrat, my first match of the tour. I made 41 in the first innings before getting caught in the gully off a backfoot forcing shot and 37 in the second when picked up at short leg. On neither occasion had I batted as long as I wanted nor as long as skipper Geoff Miller — leading England for the first time — had wanted me to. He had told me before both innings to stay as long as possible and have a good look at the Caribbean conditions.

In my first innings I had also been stuck on 37 for some time immediately following the introduction of the spinners into the Leeward Island attack but I was not concerned. Remembering Geoff's words, I was in no hurry, perfectly content to wait for the odd loose ball. Although I probably should have batted longer in each innings, I was happy with the way I played considering my lack of practice.

The Test match was vastly different. I was glad that cricket is played in long trousers otherwise the whole 14,000 plus in the Antiguan Recreation Ground would certainly have seen my legs shaking whenever I shaped up to receive the bowling. I had never felt so nervous, not even when I made my Test debut at Lord's in the Centenary Test in front of 25,000 people which should have imposed far more pressure. Yet I was deeply conscious of my legs shaking and how wobbly I felt. I still can't explain why. Like everybody else, I feel tense when I first go in to bat but never to that extent. I didn't have a chance to get over those nerves either before Colin Croft dismissed me in both innings, caught in the slips both times off rather tentative strokes.

I gathered after my innings I had caused some talk among the rest of the players and the English cricket writers because

I soon discarded my crash helmet in the second innings despite their fast bowlers. I don't particularly like batting in a helmet and seldom do at home although it is only commonsense to use one against Michael Holding and company when the conditions demand one. In Antigua however I felt more comfortable without one at that stage of the game. To make the ball get up on a four day old wicket their fast bowlers had to dig it in pretty short and I felt that my grandmother could have ducked out of the way without any trouble.

The only part of the match I enjoyed was the fielding, when I moved from the short leg position. I was soon handed the role as I was when I first got into the Yorkshire side although I don't field there nowadays. I much prefer the cover area where I can run about. Nobody really enjoys fielding at short leg with the danger of being hit and where helmets are essential. Being made to field there was a 'penalty' for joining the tour late. It is usually thrust on the newcomer to a side with the senior players 'pulling rank.' I hope I can look forward to the day when I've earned sufficient stripes for England to be able to pull rank on another newcomer.

11 ROLAND BUTCHER (MIDDLESEX & ENGLAND)

Barbados *v.* England (One Day Match)
5 March
Barbados *v.* England
7–10 March

Roland Butcher, who was born in Barbados, tells of his excitement at returning as a member of the English team and of his Test debut in the third Test.

I had not noticed skipper Ian Botham walking towards me on the Kensington Oval Test ground in Bridgetown, Barbados — some fourteen miles from where I was born — on the eve of the third Test against the West Indies. If I had, I would not have paid any special attention to his movements at that moment.

The official practice session had finished some minutes before. Not being completely happy with my form after all the interruptions we had encountered on the tour, I had stayed behind to get in an extra net session as I had done on several previous occasions. I was aware that the skipper was still somewhere on the outfield and that he had been talking with the rest of the tour selectors. It meant that he had to pass very close to me to get back to the dressing room.

He was still some yards away when he called me over, stretched out his hand and said, 'You're playing tomorrow. Well done and congratulations.' It was as simple as that. The moment I had been dreaming of since I first picked up a cricket bat and became besotted with the game as a youngster at East Point, St Phillip on the southern tip of the island, had come true.

My chance as a Test cricketer had arrived. In those early days, of course, I had dreamed of playing for the West Indies. For the previous six months, I had dreamed of playing for

England. And now the moment had arrived. It didn't matter to me that the Test was actually in Barbados itself, the country of my birth although that naturally added a final romantic twist to the dramatic change in my life the last ten months had brought. The important thing as far as I was concerned was actually being named in a Test team. It would not have mattered where the match was being played.

The rest of that day Thursday 12 March, just seemed to vanish. There were the congratulations from the rest of the party, congratulations shared with Robin Jackman who had also been named to make his Test debut at the age of thirty-five. It was a magic moment for him as well.

There was a brief moment to enjoy the news with my wife Cheryl who had flown out from England seven days earlier to join me. Then the press, radio and television interviews before I was almost overwhelmed with calls from my many friends and relatives on the island. The team dinner — an official and traditional function on the eve of a Test match — followed before another interview and then a chance to shut my hotel door, sit back and take in all that had happened.

I thought I stood a chance of playing after making 43 and 32 in the drawn game against Barbados immediately prior to the Test match. I know they are modest scores but in the context of the whole match, the wicket conditions and the strength of the bowling opposition, they bore comparison with the runs anybody else had made in the game. But I was not counting on anything. My approach to life is fairly basic and simple. I never try to anticipate anything. In that way I avoid disappointment if things should not go in my favour. It also means that I can take the goods things without appearing to jump over the moon. Yet I must admit I felt a certain tingling sensation inside me when Ian offered his hand that Thursday lunchtime.

The previous season at home with Middlesex I had started the summer with only one ambition — to gain a regular place in the Middlesex side. After five summers in the game on the Middlesex staff I had still not achieved that ranking and I believed that was all I could look forward to in 1980. Playing Test cricket was still a long way from my thoughts in those days, especially playing for England.

The summer was almost two thirds over when that prospect entered my life. With encouragement from Mike Brearley, the Middlesex and former England captain, when I did break into the championship side, I had made two scores of over 150, against Hampshire and Yorkshire. Then came the letter which was to change my life. A simple letter asking if I would be available to tour the West Indies in the winter with England. I gave it considerable thought before finally answering 'yes'. Everyway I looked at the situation my decision made sense even if some people back in the West Indies might not have understood it although nobody ever challenged me about it on the tour.

England had, after all, become my home. I had lived more than half my life in the country after arriving in 1967 to join my parents who had set up home in Stevenage, Hertfordshire. My future was going to be in England rather than the West Indies. So was the future of my two year old son Paul. They were my main considerations but there was another. If I was to be selected for England I thought it important to show thousands of other young coloured people in England it was possible to succeed in the country. At the time the letter arrived, the dole queues were growing, many young coloured people were out of work and wondering what the future held for them. My selection would show that when the better times returned, it would be possible to make progress if they tried hard enough.

When my first selection came for the second one day international against Australia at Edgbaston I found no difficulty slipping into the England side and the whole atmosphere. The rest of the players knew me, knew what I was capable of doing and accepted me as a cricketer. Being selected for the tour party was the next big moment in my life. I was actually away in Canada holidaying with relatives when it was announced but a newspaper soon tracked me down and broke the news to me.

I was soon aware when I returned home to London that I was a figure of some considerable curiosity but I accepted that. I felt it even more wherever we landed in the West Indies. On each island the official reception committees were waiting to greet us. There were other 'reception committees' such as airport workers who looked at me long and hard, fingers pointed. But never a hostile glare or word. Many hands were thrust in my direction as I walked through airport terminals.

I was prepared for all that. What I did not appreciate was how difficult touring can be for international cricket teams especially these days now that the length of stay has been cut to a bare minimum. You seem to fly in, play a game of cricket and fly out again with little rest in between, a constant routine of packing and unpacking and very little time to relax. I had been on tours before with Middlesex but they were usually concentrated on one place with very little moving around.

It was much harder than I anticipated, far more demanding than many people realise. It also brought home to me how easy it is to forget things. My wife Cheryl has a hard time getting me out of bed in England, especially in the winter when I'm not playing cricket. After fourteen years in England I still haven't adjusted to the cold, one of the reasons why I was not too keen on furthering my football career as a part time professional when I had the opportunity. Although I had spent the early part of my life in Barbados living with my grandmother Marie Stuart and visited the island every winter for the last seven years, I'd forgotten how everything seems to wake up with the dawn and it is almost impossible to sleep once the sun comes streaming down. It meant early nights to get enough sleep.

During our stop over in Barbados on our outward journey from London to Antigua, I had managed to slip out of the airport to see my grandmother and other relatives. My grandmother, who virtually brought me up for the first thirteen years of my life while my parents were establishing a home in England, is a fantastic old lady. She's seventy-five years of age and still very active. I doubt if there is a job of work a man can do that she can't do now even at her age. One of the greatest treats of the tour was my first Sunday in Barbados and going home for a typical Bajan Sunday lunch she had cooked for me. It was almost ample compensation for leaving Georgetown, Guyana early when the second Test had to be called off following the deportation order against Robin Jackman.

The whole affair saddened me because the game of cricket suffered. Not only did we suffer as players but hundreds of people suffered too, denied the chance to watch a Test match they had been looking forward to for months. Whatever the strength of the side, there is always something special about an England side in the Caribbean. When things like that happen I always try to take the view that they happen for the best and that something good will result from it.

The most upsetting part of the Guyana leg from a purely personal view was being denied a chance of playing a decent innings when rain washed out the four day fixture against Guyana. People keep telling me that the Bourda wicket is good for batting but I've never had a chance to find out. Twice I've been due to play there and each time the game has been cancelled.

In 1976 I returned to Barbados for the winter and managed to break into the Barbados side for the Shell Shield. I was selected for the match against Guyana in Georgetown but that was called off on the first morning because of objections to Geoffrey Greenidge in the Barbados team. Geoffrey, the former Sussex and West Indies opening batsman, had played cricket in South Africa. The Barbados Crickt Association refused to withdraw him from the side and we were ordered home.

This time the weather denied me a chance which meant that I arrived in Barbados to make my bid for a Test place with only one first class match behind me plus three one day innings including the two one day internationals in St Vincent and Berbice. Every time I had batted on the tour I had been in a position where runs were wanted quickly leaving me little or no time to settle down and build an innings with some care.

In Pointe-a-Pierre I had gone into bat against the Young West Indies side knowing that Ian was looking for a declaration total. In the one day matches, of course, it is essential to get on with the game. I came off once, in the first match against the Windward Islands in St Vincent when I batted number three which gave me a little more time to settle and finished with 44, the highest on our side. In the two one day internationals I went in at number five without too much success.

I'm afraid I didn't distinguish myself in my first match in Barbados either, the hastily arranged one day fixture against a Barbados XI to give us much needed practice after the Governments of Barbados, Antigua, Jamaica and Montserrat had given us the go ahead to continue the tour. Apart from Desmond Haynes and Malcolm Marshall, we found ourselves up against the full Barbados team. All their main bowlers, Sylvester Clarke, Wayne Daniel, Joel Garner, Collis King and their skipper Albert Padmore were Test bowlers. It was a tough way to re-start the tour but just the right type of opposition we needed to get us thinking cricket again. Our 11 run victory was a great boost to our spirits.

Graham Gooch once again dominated our innings when we were put in. Two days earlier in a private practice match on the same wicket he had scored a century and looked as though he would score another one until he hit his wicket attempting to hook Garner when he was 16 short of his 100. He had played well against the faster bowlers in keeping them out and then really opened up against Padmore's off spin, hitting him for 21 in one over including two sixes. There was a constant noise all around the ground while Graham was batting. Workmen seemed to be everywhere with hammers, drills, welding equipment, saws etc putting the finishing touches to the ground in readiness for the Test. Perhaps Graham felt completely at home because he is a keen do-it-yourself expert.

Mike Gatting and David Gower also played well and I was the only one of the first six batsmen who failed to get into double figures. Again I went in when we were searching for runs quickly just as Wayne and Sylvester were brought back to their final flings. I had made nine when Wayne removed my middle stump—hardly the way to treat a fellow Barbadian and Middlesex colleague!

Possibly my worst moments were to come in the field just when Barbados were closing in on our total of 207 for 6 off 50 overs. After a poor start which saw Graham Stevenson removed, Gordon Greenidge and Emmerson Trotman and Ian account for Alvin Greenidge, Barbados threatened victory when the Reifer brothers, George and Leslie plus Collis King took the score from 25 for 3 to 158 for 6. I was guilty of dropping both George and Leslie. They were both simple catches half way back to the boundary. I just didn't pick up the first from George until it was too late and the second came out of the background of the long, low stand which runs along one side of the Kensington Oval ground.

Most people were kind enough to put it down to nerves, the pressure I was under making my first appearance for England in Barbados. That just was not true. I certainly did not feel under any pressure. In fact I felt very comfortable playing there, a ground I knew well, conditions I had enjoyed in the past. Almost as comfortable playing at Lord's for Middlesex. If I get worried at all, it is when I play on grounds I don't know.

Although Barbados still had some powerful hitters to come in Clarke, Daniel and Garner, the target proved beyond them once the Reifer brothers and Collis had fallen. They needed 66 off the last 10 overs and did well in getting to within 11 runs. If we needed a boost at the critical stage when the runs were coming quite quickly, most of the team got one with about 20 overs to go when a British Airways Jumbo flew almost over the ground. They stopped and waved for they knew that on board were the wives of most of the players. I had to wait another twenty-four hours before Cheryl arrived.

At the end of that game I wouldn't have given too much for my chances of playing in the Test match. I knew the four day game against Barbados was going to make or break me. The afternoon before that match Bill Athey had arrived from Australia and there was some thought of rushing him straight into the side which meant that I would probably have been the one to go. Fortunately for me, the selectors thought it was expecting too much of Bill after a journey from Sydney that had taken him more than a day.

If I wasn't happy with my form, I knew the selectors could not have been. They may not have been too impressed by me in the nets either. I am not a good net player. I'm quite willing to practice for long hours but I do find them a bit of a chore, lacking in challenge when there are no fielders around. There is not the same feeling of satisfaction hitting the ball into a side netting even when everything connects perfectly as there is in splitting the field or even hitting one over the top.

I had another worry too. My old faithful Slazenger bat, which I have used for the last three years and had with me when I made those two large scores for Middlesex in the 1980 summer which first attracted the attention of the England selectors, was in danger of coming apart. There was so much tape holding it together that it was heavier than it should have been. I should have had it repaired but I was afraid that if anything was done to it, the bat would be affected in some way.

A batsman often builds up a special relationship with one particular bat. They all look alike. Yet they are all so different. The balance, the feel, even the noise it makes must be just right. I trusted this one particular bat. With this one bat I knew that when I went to hit a spinner over the top, the ball would go over the top even if I mishit it a little. It's a faith I don't have in any other bat at the moment although I've got a collection.

I used it in the first innings against Barbados when I made 43, an innings I was criticised for. In the second innings I borrowed Peter Willey's bat and made 32. I was praised for the way I played then. It's strange how it works out. But I went back to old trusty for the Test match.

Many people watching the Barbados game found it boring. Even some seasoned former players said they could not understand the tactics and found it strange that the batsmen did not make a greater effort to score faster. There was nothing strange about it. The wicket conditions and the bowling just didn't allow for it. There is a little more grass on the wicket in Barbados these days compared to the time I played on it. Quite a fair degree of bounce as well for the first couple of days. In Marshall, Daniel, Clarke and King, Barbados had four bowlers who knew how to get the most out of it even on the final day when they bowled — in the main — off shortened runs. The occasional ball was also keeping low. It was not a wicket for stroke making.

In England's case there was also a great need to get in some batting practice, making the most of our last chance before the third Test match. It was the first of the tour where we had come across an attack similar to the one we had to face in the Test and based on pure pace. Unfortunately Graham

Gooch, Mike Gatting and David Gower were all out before they could get going which took me in to join Geoff Boycott who batted 273 minutes on that first day for his 77 runs. It was a brave and determined innings against a lot of shortish bowling which meant that he had to be very patient in waiting for the odd delivery he could hit.

I lost him as a partner when he was caught at mid-on driving against Padmore but failing to get hold of the ball properly. Several people suggested I should have fallen long before I did because I played far too many 'air' shots.

Criticism of that type doesn't upset me although it can be a little annoying. I don't see anything wrong in playing the ball uppishly and in the air as long as it is safe and away from the fielders. Viv Richards plays many of them and few people complain about his batting. What matters more to me is the number of runs you finish with. Previously on this tour people had talked quite a lot about David Gower's 187 in the first match at Pointe-a-Pierre not mentioning the fact he was dropped half a dozen times. In the first innings against Barbados I scored 43 and only Geoff and Peter Willey who reached 51 on the second morning scored more in our innings of 298 although Ian made a useful 40 and David Bairstow chipped out 22 runs. I was out as many people expected me to be out, caught by Gordon Greenidge who held a catch at deep mid-on.

Apart from Gordon Greenidge and Desmond Haynes, the Barbados side found scoring runs as difficult as we had done. Gordon and Desmond opened up in their usual style. They had 50 on the board in 10 overs and Barbados scored their first 100 in the twenty-eighth. Gordon fell at that score when he was caught at first slip driving against John Emburey, Desmond having already been dismissed giving a catch behind against Robin Jackman. From then on Barbados were forced to proceed with caution in making their 334.

I was pleased for both John and Robin who turned out to be our most successful bowlers. Robin was playing his first match since his arrival caused the controversy and quickly showed the value of his experience by his controlled line and strength in finishing with four wickets. John's performance was startling. He went into the attack half an hour before tea on the second afternoon and got through 49.4 overs before he finished off the innings half an hour after tea on the third afternoon. The only rest he had during that time bowling from the pavilion end was when the new ball was taken and that lasted no more than half an hour.

He thoroughly deserved his five wickets and I was glad to help him taking catches off successive deliveries to dismiss David Murray and Padmore. They helped me forget the two I had put down in the one day match and neither of them was so easy. As in that one day game, George Reifer, at nineteen one of the most promising players in Barbados, and King proved the main stumbling blocks in scoring 71 and 76 respectively.

With Barbados gaining just a 36 run lead and only seven hours left to play, there did not seem any danger of us suffering an embarassing defeat just before the Test yet such a danger emerged on the last day. Boycott received a ball from Clarke which rose up nastily and he was caught at second slip. Graham Gooch was caught behind off one from Daniel which cut away at the last second and Mike Gatting was completely beaten by Marshall when the ball crept all along the ground after pitching. We were only 47 ahead at that stage when I went to the wicket to join David Gower and I was lucky to survive my first ball. Just like the one to Mike, it never rose more than a few inches and I just managed to drop my bat on it at the last moment.

It wasn't a time for any heroics although I did pull Daniel for six. In the circumstances my one intention was to show that I was quite capable of surviving and spent almost two hours over my 32 runs before I was beaten off the wicket and fell leg before to Marshall. We were still not completely safe then especially with Ian giving a catch behind two balls later but David, Peter Willey and David Bairstow made sure there were no further alarms as we scored 219 for 6 when play finished.

There was a free day the next day to go through plus the net session on the Thursday morning before that moment arrived when Ian called me to him. The photographers made a fuss on the first day of the Test when I walked out with the England team to field. It was the proudest cricketing moment of my life with my grandmother Marie and my wife Cheryl watching from the stand along with relatives and friends who had flown in from England, Canada and the United States hoping to combine a holiday and see my play in a Test.

But that proud moment was overtaken by an even greater one on the second day when I walked down the pavilion steps of the Pickwick Club and on to the outfield. It seemed that everybody in the ground which must have numbered almost fifteen thousand stood up to applaud me on, black and white together. Not just Barbadians either because groups had flown in from several of the smaller islands around as well as Trinidad and Jamaica.

It was a very touching moment for me. And very sad when I look back to think that less than twenty-four hours later the whole crowd in the Kensington Oval was on its feet once more, this time in complete silence paying tribute to Ken Barrington who had died the previous night. Obviously I shall never forget my first Test match but the memory will never be the happy one it should have been.

BARBADOS *v.* ENGLAND (one day match)
BRIDGETOWN, MARCH 5

England		
G. Boycott	c Murray b King	14
G. A. Gooch	hit wkt b Garner	84
M. W. Gatting	b King	25
D. I. Gower	c Murray b Garner	39
R. O. Butcher	b Daniel	9
*I. T. Botham	b Daniel	12
P. Willey	not out	1
+D. L. Bairstow	not out	6
Extras	b 5, lb 11, nb 1	17
Total	50 overs 6 wickets	207

Fall of wickets: 1—30, 2—97, 3—159, 4—178, 5—200, 6—201
J. E. Emburey, G. B. Stevenson and C. M. Old did not bat

Bowling: Clarke 10—4—14—0; Daniel 10—2—34—2; Garner 10—0—38—2; King 10--2—37—2; Padmore 9—1—58—0; L. Reifer 1—0—9—0.

Barbados

C. G. Greenidge	c Old b Stevenson	1
T. Greenidge	lbw b Botham	9
E. Trotman	c Gatting b Stevenson	9
G. Reifer	c Willey b Botham	55
L. King	b Willey	43
L. Reifer	c Emburey b Botham	38
T. Clarke	b Botham	4
J. Garner	c Botham b Stevenson	9
+D. A. Murray	b Stevenson	8
*A. Padmore	b Old	13
W. W. Daniel	not out	2
Extras	lb 3, nb 2	5
Total	49.3 overs	196

Fall of wickets: 1—1, 2—15, 3—25, 4—92, 5—158, 6—158, 7—164, 8—177, 9—185

Bowling: Botham 10—2—30—4; Stevenson 10—2—38—4; Gooch 6—0—31—0; Old 5.3—0—29—1; Emburey 9—2—40—0; Willey 9—3—23—1

* captain + wicket-keeper

England won by 11 runs

BARBADOS *v.* ENGLAND
BRIDGETOWN, 7–10 MARCH

England

	First Innings		*Second Innings*	
G. A. Gooch	b Clarke	18	c Murray b Daniel	29
G. Boycott	c Trotman b Padmore	77	c King b Clarke	13
M. W. Gatting	c Murray b Marshall	11	b Marshall	22
D. I. Gower	run out	18	c Clarke b Padmore	44
R. O. Butcher	c Greenidge b Padmore	43	lbw b Marshall	32
*I. T. Botham	c Murray b Padmore	40	c Murray b Marshall	0
P. Willey	c Murray b Clarke	51	not out	34
D. L. Bairstow	run out	22	not out	26
G. B. Stevenson	b Clarke	2		
R. D. Jackman	b Padmore	5		
J. Emburey	not out			
Extras	b 2, lb 2, nb 7	11	b 9, lb 9, nb 1	19
Total		298	(six wickets dec.)	219

Fall of wickets: 1—24, 2—47, 3—92, 4—168, 5—179, 6—252, 7—282, 8—285, 9—294.
1—35, 2—63, 3—83, 4—144, 5—144, 6—168

Bowling: First innings — Clarke 35—9—67—3; Daniel 27—4—82—0; Marshall 19—6—42—1; King 13—2—25—0; Padmore 38.4—10—71—4. Second innings: Clarke 24—6—55—1, Marshall 18—7—25—3; Daniel 22—5—51—1; Padmore 22—5—51—1; King 7—3—9—0; G. Reifer 1—0—7—0; D. Haynes 1—0—2—0.

Barbados

C. G. Greenidge	c Botham b Emburey	45
D. L. Haynes	c Bairstow b Jackman	44
G. Reifer	c Gower b Jackman	71
E. Trotman	c Botham b Emburey	10
C. L. King	lbw b Botham	76
L. Reifer	c Bairstow b Jackman	4
+D. A. Murray	c Butcher b Emburey	19
M. D. Marshall	not out	29
*A. L. Padmore	c Butcher b Emburey	0
T. Clarke	b Jackman	0
W. W. Daniel	b Emburey	21
Extras	b 2, lb 8, w 1, nb 4	15
Total		334

Fall of wickets: 1—83, 2—100, 3—124, 4—254, 5—262, 6—269, 7—296, 8—296, 9—296

Bowling: Botham 24—6—79—1; Stevenson 13—2—66—0; Emburey 49.4—13—92—5; Jackman 25—6—68—4; Willey 10—4—14—0

* captain + wicket-keeper

Match drawn

12 GRAHAM GOOCH (ESSEX & ENGLAND)

Third Test

13–18 March

Graham Gooch scored his second Test century in the third Test but as he says, this was completely overshadowed for the whole team with the tragic death of Ken Barrington.

I shall never be able to look back on my second Test century with any pleasure. A great deal of personal satisfaction, certainly; but never pleasure. It is a bare statistic in the record books. Another statistic stuck in my memory. But one that will always be associated with pain and tragedy emerging from the saddest game of cricket I've ever played.

The third Test of the series in Bridgetown, Barbados will never be remembered for the century I scored in our second innings, the centuries of Clive Lloyd and Viv Richards in West Indies 298 run victory or the first time that a black West Indian played in a Test match for England as Roland Butcher did.

No, it will always be associated with the heart attack late on the second day which robbed cricket of one of its greatest characters and one of the finest men I have known when it took our assistant manager Ken Barrington away from us. It was a shock and a loss we felt for the rest of the tour. One we never recovered from on the most ill fated tour cricket could have known.

We knew it was going to be a struggle to save the match following our disastrous first innings of 122 before Ken died. But his death didn't help our fight for survival although everybody did their best to earn a draw to serve the memory of Ken who played so many brave innings in lost causes for England. Every member of the team was in bed before Ken died about forty minutes to midnight and nobody knew until the following morning.

I answered a gentle tap on my hotel room door at 7.30 in

the morning and instinctively knew something was wrong when I opened it to find manager Alan Smith and captain Ian Botham standing there. They gave me the sad news and then passed on down the hotel corridors knocking up the rest of the team. It must have been the most soul destroying walk either of them had taken.

There were tears in the eyes of most of the team as we paid our own private tribute to Ken, collecting together for a minute's silence on the pier jutting out into the Caribbean sea from our hotel. More tears, too, when we lined up for a minute's silence before the start of the third day's play.

It was probably just as well we were in the field on that Sunday as the West Indies carried on their second innings building on their 143 run lead. It meant the team was forced to concentrate on their cricket and force the tragedy out of their minds. They did a thoroughly professional job in the circumstances even managing to keep Viv Richards subdued for long periods of time and the runs down to 239 in the day on what was, by then, a fairly innocuous wicket with our pace attack operating on it. Even so it was obvious to everybody that nobody was particularly enjoying their work that day.

I was not so fortunate. I had split a finger on my right hand on Saturday morning when taking part in slip catching practice before the start. I couldn't field because of the danger of another knock which might have widened the split and prevented me batting a second time. All I could do was sit in the dressing room area of the Pickwick Cricket Club on the Kensington Oval ground and watch. It gave me plenty of time to think of what Ken had meant to me in particular, the team in general and everybody associated with England.

He was more than an assistant manager in charge of the cricket side, a man who bowled in the nets until everybody was finished, then took part in giving slip catches. He organised the laundry, generally looked after us on and off the field. He was always ready to listen to the problems of anybody. His room door was never closed. I owe him a lot, particularly on the tour to Australia the previous winter after I had been left out of the side for the first Test in Perth. He spent some time building up my confidence, instilling in me the need to bat for a long time, never waste a chance to cash in when the ball was running my way.

'Remember,' he told me 'it is criminal to throw away a chance of a big score when the opportunity is there. One big score may easily be followed by a run of little ones and you'll be glad of that big score to fall back on.' They were sound words I remembered when I batted for England in the second innings and made my second Test century. I think Ken would have been proud of me that day; I hope so.

I felt that score was in me. I felt that I could take on the West Indies fast bowlers once I had managed to survive the new ball when anything can happen. Despite the constant interruptions to our programme by rain and the Guyana affair, the dreadful lack of practice facilities which was disgraceful and the shortage of visits to the crease in first class matches, I felt in fairly good nick. Not as good as the previous summer when I scored my first Test century against them at Lord's in entirely different circumstances, but good enough to have a go.

Not that I expected England to win the Test match in Barbados on a wicket which appeared to have been specially prepared for the West Indies pace attack. It wasn't doctored in the way pitches have sometimes been changed overnight in mysterious circumstances but there is no doubt in my mind that the wicket was prepared just to suit them and not us. In much the same way some county sides at home prepare wickets to suit their own bowlers rather than the opposition. It's part and parcel of the game and happens all over the world except in England where we seem to go to extraordinary lengths to prepare a fair wicket whatever moans the Australians have made in the past.

I wasn't hopeful of winning because I thought the task was beyond us. It's not being defeatist, only realistic when you compared the two teams involved. To beat the West Indies I believe we need to make a score in the region of 500 in our first innings to be able to apply any pressure. Even if two or three batsmen came off together, they bowl their overs so slowly with their four man pace attack that it would take us almost two and a half days to score that many runs. Then we would have the task of bowling the West Indies out twice in the remaining half of the match. We would need all the luck going to be able to do that. Luck was not our companion.

The West Indies had naturally kept the same side which won the first Test by an innings and 79 runs. We made four changes from the rather ill balanced side we had taken into the Trinidad match. We played a much stronger batting side for Barbados although it didn't make much difference in the end. Mike Gatting came in at number three for the unfortunate Brian Rose, Roland Butcher at number five for Geoff Miller, David Bairstow returned behind the wickets and Robin Jackman took over from Chris Old.

Brian Rose's replacement Bill Athey had flown in but he was not given a chance to compete for a place in the side which I thought was a mistake. He had arrived from Australia the day before the four day match against Barbados, a tiring journey across America. Yet I thought that Athey should have played in that match especially as he was then the only one in the party with any real experience of batting number three. He has a sound technique against fast bowlers and if he had played against Barbados it would have given the tour selectors another option for the Test. Bill was keen to play and there was no acclimatisation problem as far as he was concerned having been playing in the heat of Australia for three months.

I was pleased about Robin's first Test cap. He has been a wholehearted trier in county cricket for a number of years and has troubled me on more than one occasion in Essex/ Surrey matches. Yet, in a way, it was rather sad that he should have been given a chance by the other two pace bowlers, Graham Stevenson and Chris Old, who were chasing the final position. Both had been original choices for the tour, both had been thoroughly acclimatised, both knew the wicket conditions yet neither had been able to bowl convincingly enough to keep out Robin.

With all the grass on the wicket — despite almost daily appeals from Geoff Boycott to the groundsman over the previous ten days to shave more off — Ian just had to put the West Indies in when he won the toss. It has become a regular routine in Barbados. With their own four fast bowlers Barbados always put the opposition in these days in Shell

Shield matches. There is always going to be life and bounce on the first day. Our attack needed every assistance it can get to bowl the West Indies out, even a West Indies side which is suspect in batting in the odd places.

We got it that first morning. Before the match was a hundred minutes old, the first four West Indies batsmen had been shot out including Richards second ball for a duck. Well over two thousand Englishmen had flown into Barbados to support us and they were given something to cheer about. Unfortunately we were not able to give them much to shout about after that.

After all that had happened to him following his sixteen year wait for England to recognise his bowling talents, it was fitting that Robin Jackman should make the breakthrough with only his fifth ball in Test cricket. He took over after Gordon Greenidge and Desmond Haynes had taken 24 off the first seven overs and with that fifth delivery had Greenidge pushing forward just outside his off stump only for the ball to find the edge and finish up in my hands. A simple, straightforward catch as first slip catches go but nice to feel nestling safely in my hands all the same.

Just one over later and the whole ground was in uproar as Graham Dilley came charging in against Richards. He waved his bat at the ball fairly unconvincingly and Ian took a fine one handed catch to his left, a magnificent effort. The West Indies were 25 for 2, soon to be 65 for 4.

Off the first ball of his sixth over Robin dismissed Haynes when he had him caught behind and Botham, never to be outdone in these situations when wickets are tumbling, returned to have Everton Mattis out leg before, a plumb decision even though the tall, young Jamaican seemed reluctant to leave the wicket. That was the end of our runaway success as Clive Lloyd promoted himself one place up the order in an attempt to stop the slide and found just the partner he needed in Larry Gomes during a 154 run stand for the fifth wicket which really destroyed our hopes on that wicket. Most days we would have been grateful to have settled for having the West Indies on 238 for seven at the close of play but when taking into consideration our start, we probably should have been looking for an all out total of less than two hundred even allowing for one man settling down for a while.

Clive did that superbly. If we could have forced him into serious error, the whole outcome might have been different. But we also have to face the fact that we just haven't got the attack with enough pace in it to keep going as the West Indies can do. Dilley is the only pure pace bowler we have and, at twenty-one, he is still learning his trade. We just didn't have the ammunition to come back and throw at Clive in the afternoon when he produced some magnificent driving on his way to his fourteenth Test century. Gomes was the weak link in the all left handed partnership. He offered a catch and a stumping chance behind the wicket against John Emburey which David Bairstow was not able to accept on what was undoubtedly his unhappiest session for England.

We got them both out before the close when we hit back in the last forty-five minutes of the day. Clive was caught at square leg, another simple catch straight to me as he attempted to drive Jackman, Gomes went to second slip and Bairstow got some satisfaction from the day when he caught David Murray.

Limiting the West Indies to 238 for 7 still gave us a chance. Getting the last three wickets for 27 runs on the second morning and dismissing them for 265 was satisfactory if we could bat reasonably well ourselves. We never had a chance from the time Michael Holding struck in his first over. He is an astonishing bowler. He slips right into his rhythm from the first delivery and doesn't need two or three balls to warm up. Clive Lloyd said during the match that he believed Holding was bowling faster during this series than he had ever done. It might have been a propaganda move but Geoff Boycott would not argue with him.

The first five balls Geoff faced from Holding were almost unplayable. I think he managed to get a bat on one, possibly two but the rest just beat him for sheer pace aided by some lift and movement off the wicket. The sixth beat him completely to send his off stump out of the ground. For a moment Geoff stood there in sheer disbelief before sadly shaking his head and walking away.

We just lost wickets regularly after that. Apart from

Boycott and myself plus last man Dilley, the rest were caught in the arc between wicket-keeper and gully which gives a clue as to how the West Indies bowled. I wouldn't have backed any side to have scored 200 against them on that wicket and it is annoying when you hear that our performance was described as pathetic by some people. If you were fortunate enough to settle in, then it was possible to score runs but they were still capable of producing the odd delivery at any moment which is virtually unplayable.

It is a remarkable bowling attack they possess at the moment as their record must surely prove. They are not unintelligent either. There was some muttering from England supporters that they bowled too many bouncers. You don't often see them bowling bouncers these days. They bowled nothing like the number Andy Roberts and Holding bowled during the 1976 summer. Not the type that go over your head.

They have all developed the knack of getting the ball to rise at you off just short of a length so that you are forced to play it from somewhere under your chin. But that is not a bouncer in the old meaning of the word. When the wicket is in their favour, they are going to bowl you out, make no mistake about that. When it is not helping them, they are not going to give you anything either. It's sheer hard work which needs luck and determination as well as skill to stay in against them for any reasonable length of time.

I think there is another factor that many people overlook. Against most Test attacks the tail end batsmen can usually contribute 50 or 60 runs to the side's score which often has an important bearing on the result. Just in the way the West Indies did against us in the first Test in Trinidad which made all the difference. Without those extra runs from Andy Roberts and the rest, they would not have been able to make us follow on in Port of Spain. But when batting against them, you can't really expect our tail enders to survive for very long. Their pace bowlers clean-up tail enders for a pastime.

The over after Holding had dismissed Boycott, we had another setback when Mike Gatting was caught in the slips against Roberts. For a while David Gower and I managed to hang around and I thought we had got over the worst part when I was out. I was very disappointed with my dismissal for I had managed to see off the new ball and it was my time to cash in. Big Joel Garner stopped me. The ball before I had let go outside my off stump but it must have moved back a long way off the wicket judging by the anguished looks on the faces of the West Indies slip fielders who couldn't understand why I had not been bowled. The next ball was a similar delivery bowled just a little straighter which tucked me up as I went to play it only to chop it on to my wicket.

From then on the slips were kept pretty busy as we slipped to 122 all out, some 143 runs behind, in less than five hours. It was so frustrating trying to stay in against them that Botham even threw his bat away after one delivery from Holding which he said later he couldn't understand where it came from. It was only just short of a length yet it went through him about chin high. 'How it got up like that I'll never know unless they have put a well sprung mattress under the wicket,' he said.

I could understand his disappointment. He was out, in fact, to the very next delivery, another which took off and he was caught behind trying to fend it away. Yet I thought his act of throwing the bat down was a little silly coming from the captain. It was hardly the way to encourage the lesser batsmen to follow although they were expected to stay at the wicket and play such deliveries if possible.

The only man who did survive for any length of time apart from the captain and myself was Peter Willey who spent 125 minutes over his unbeaten 19 with mainly the tail enders for company. He is a very gutsy player who stands up to the fast bowlers with tremendous courage. He hasn't made the number of runs for England he might have been expected to make but going in at number seven he is generally at the crease around the time the second new ball is taken. As I said earlier, against this attack the new ball is always likely to produce two or three wickets.

Unfortunately that score of 122 was the last look Ken Barrington had of English cricket for it was later that evening that he suffered his heart attack in his hotel bedroom soon after going to bed. If that wasn't enough, we were also being pestered by a silly Yorkshireman who thought it was great fun to ring us up any time during the night and complain about the way we were playing.

He caught Kenny and Ian as well as our manager until Smith asked the hotel switchboard not to put through any calls to the rooms of players between ten in the evening and eight in the morning. Unfortunately Alan had to accept every call because of his position and it wasn't pleasant being woken at four in the morning to have a lot of abuse hurled at you. At first we thought he was phoning from Yorkshire but then he gave himself away by his stupid boasting in a bar one evening and we were able to identify him. He was spotted sitting on the boundary edge of the match on the final day and Peter Willey along with Bernard Thomas brought him to the dressing room where he was given the biggest dressing down he has ever received. Cricket can do without idiots like him.

The only thing that went our way on the Saturday was Dilley trapping Greenidge leg before which meant they started on six for one on the Sunday morning following the two minutes' silence for Ken. That was an impressive tribute, all fifteen thousand people in the ground standing, black and white together and everybody silent, even the youngsters who never saw Ken play and may not even have heard of him. Perhaps they sensed the sadness enveloped the whole ground.

Watching from the dressing room because of my hand injury I thought we did a sound job in the field throughout the day. We gave them very little and they never broke loose although Colin Croft performed well for them having gone in as night watchman on the Saturday. He stayed to see the shine off the new ball as well as making his highest Test score of 33 before he mistimed a drive to mid-off.

He left a perfect opening for Viv Richards with the shine gone, the wicket playing more easily and the West Indies under no pressure having a near 200 run lead at that stage. Although Viv just managed to get his century off the last over of the day, he was never allowed to play with complete freedom.

Mind you he was determined to get that century. The Kensington Oval is not one of his favourite run scoring grounds and he had a long history of batting failures in Barbados both in Test cricket and the Shell Shield. He wanted to make up for them. And he did by making his highest Test score in the Caribbean before the West Indies declared 522 on leaving us five full sessions to survive.

That was on the fourth day. On the third day, the Sunday, we had kept them in check even though we managed to take only four wickets before the close. Desmond Haynes did not last long before falling leg before to Botham, Everton Mattis played a poor stroke to be caught in the covers against Robin Jackman and Larry Gomes finally ran himself out as he had often threatened to do during his 82 run partnership with Richards for the fifth wicket. The only question to be answered before the close was whether Richards would complete his century. His timing, as usual, was perfect pulling Dilley for four to reach three figures off the last but one ball of the day.

On the rest day Clive let it be known that he was looking for a 500 run lead before he declared. He is not one for declaring if he can help it, preferring to let his side go on and on, squeezing the last breath of hope out of the opposition and I thought he went on too long on the fourth morning.

He has complete faith in his fast bowlers to be able to blast out any opposition whatever the wicket conditions. And it must be said that even if the wicket is slow, the ball is still coming at you between 85 and 90 miles an hour through the air which doesn't give you much time to pick up the line and length and take the appropriate counter measures. With the freedom of knowing that even if they got out, it didn't matter, Viv and Clive tore into us on that fourth morning, their sixth wicket partnership worth 153 in 136 minutes before Clive fell leg before against Botham swinging across the line. They were 508 runs ahead then and I thought they should have declared so that they could have a go at getting one wicket before lunch. Clive decided to bat on, possibly giving Richards a chance of making a double century. Instead he was still 18 runs short when the West Indies made their lunchtime declaration.

With the way the wicket was playing at that time I thought we had a good chance of saving the match. I still thought so even when we had lost Boycott and Gatting with our innings only two overs old. With his fifth ball of the innings Holding made one fly again to catch Boycott on the hand, the ball lobbing to Garner in the gully. The next ball Gatting had also gone, bowled by a delivery which hardly got off the ground when he had every right to expect to be playing it around his chin after seeing how the previous delivery had re-acted.

Once again — as in the first innings — I thought that David Gower and I had got over the worst and were in a position to start pulling us out of deep trouble when we added 120 together for the third wicket. David had done well on the tour, playing with more maturity than he had shown before, picking his shots with greater care, cutting out much of his bat waving outside the off stump yet still prepared to give the ball a whack if the opportunity arose. I always back a classy looking player at the highest level and David has class.

Unfortunately it wasn't to take him through that fourth day. He got to 54 by which time Lloyd had been forced to call on the off spin of Richards. David tried to cut him rather delicately without really moving his feet and played on via the bottom edge of the bat. He was desperately upset with his dismissal, feeling that he had let everybody down and, in truth, it was a poor shot.

The West Indies had been a little down when David was dismissed with thirty minutes to go before the close. It was just the fillip they needed to raise themselves again, having Botham caught at first slip for only one and almost getting me before the end of the day. When I was 71 I drove at a wider delivery from Roberts aiming square of the wicket, an area which brings me many runs but did not quite connect properly. Fortunately there was still enough power in the shot to surprise Garner in the gully and not even his gigantic left hand could close itself around the ball.

We started the last day with only five wickets left but even then I thought we might have a chance if Peter Willey and I could get through to lunch time without any major disasters. We soon had one when Willey was given out leg before against Croft, a most unfortunate decision. Willey was down the wicket when the ball struck him on the pads. Even then I did not think there was any way the ball could have hit the wicket taking into consideration his delivery from wide of the crease and the line of the ball. That was our last chance gone of saving the match especially as David Bairstow was out in the same over off the second ball he faced.

By then I had already got my century. I had started the morning on 88 not out, managed to drive Holding to the boundary, take another off Roberts through the gully region and finally reached three figures after 262 minutes when turning Holding for two to square leg. It was by no means as fluent as my first against them but in the circumstances I was still very pleased with the effort and its content. As Ken had taught me, I started to settle down for more knowing that I had the rest of the day to spare as long as I did not run out of partners. Unfortunately I was the next to go, searching for the boundary again in the gully region only this time Garner clung on to the catch as I drove against Croft. Some people may say I should not have played the shot but it is one that has rewarded me well in the past and I hit it crisply enough.

From then on it was only a matter of time before the West Indies secured their second victory of the series, one which was to mean they couldn't be beaten with only two more left. There was not even the hint of a cloud around to save us or spare the Englishmen who had turned up for the final day hoping for a miracle. They must have outnumbered the West Indians two-to-one, the local cricket enthusiasts confident the match had been won the day before.

Robin Jackman batted for fifty minutes, John Emburey stayed around for seventy-five minutes to frustrate the West Indies but the only measure of satisfaction we had on that final day was in reducing the winning margin to below 300.

Despite my century, it remains one Test match I will look back on without any pleasure. A tour, in fact, that will not spark many great memories when I look back on it in years to come. Three months in the sun during the middle of an English winter sounds very inviting but, as far as cricket tours go, this one to the West Indies was over-rated.

WEST INDIES *v.* ENGLAND (Third Test)
BARBADOS 13–18 MARCH

West Indies

	First Innings		*Second Innings*	
C.G. Greenidge	c Gooch b Jackman	14	lbw b Dilley	0
D.L. Haynes	c Bairstow b Jackman	25	lbw b Botham	25
I.V.A. Richards	c Botham b Dilley	0	not out	182
E. Mattis	lbw b Botham	16	c Butcher b Jackman	24
*C.H. Lloyd	c Gooch b Jackman	100	lbw b Botham	66
H.A. Gomes	c Botham b Dilley	58	run out	34
+D.A. Murray	c Bairstow b Dilley	9	not out	5
A.M.E. Roberts	c Bairstow b Botham	14	c Bairstow b Botham	0
J. Garner	c Bairstow b Botham	15		
M.E. Holding	c Gatting b Botham	0		
C.E.H. Croft	not out	0	c Boycott b Jackman	33
Extras	b 4, lb 6, w 2, nb 2	14	b 3, lb 7	10
Total		265	(seven wickets dec.)	379

Fall of wickets: 1—24, 2—25, 3—47, 4—65, 5—219, 6—224, 7—236, 8- 258, 9—258.
1—0, 2- 57, 3—71, 4—130, 5—212, 6—365, 7—365.

Bowling: First innings — Dilley 23—7—51—3; Botham 25.1—5—77—4; Jackman 22—4—65—3; Emburey 18—4—45—0; Gooch 2—0—13—0.
Second innings — Dilley 25—3—111—1; Botham 29—5—102—3; Jackman 25—5—76—2; Emburey 24—7—57—0; Willey 6—0—23—0.

England

	First Innings		*Second Innings*	
G. A. Gooch	b Garner	26	c Garner b Croft	116
G. Boycott	b Holding	0	c Garner b Holding	1
M. W. Gatting	c Greenidge b Roberts	2	b Holding	0
D. I. Gower	c Mattis b Croft	17	b Richards	54
R. O. Butcher	c Richards b Croft	17	lbw b Richards	2
*I. T. Botham	c Murray b Holding	26	c Lloyd b Roberts	1
P. Willey	not out	19	lbw b Croft	17
+D. L. Bairstow	c Mattis b Holding	0	c Murray b Croft	2
J. E. Emburey	c Lloyd b Roberts	0	b Garner	9
R. D. Jackman	c Roberts b Croft	7	b Garner	7
G. R. Dilley	c Gomes b Croft	0	not out	7
Extras	b 1, lb 1, nb 6	8	b 1, lb 3, nb 4	8
Total		122		224

Fall of wickets: 1—6, 2—11, 3—40, 4—55, 5—72, 6—94, 7—94, 8—97, 9—122.
1—2, 2—2, 3—122, 4—134, 5—139, 6—196, 7—198, 8—201, 9—213

Bowling: First innings — Roberts 11—3—29—2; Holding 11—7—16—3; Croft 13.5—2—39—4; Garner 12—5- 30—1.
Second innings — Roberts 20—6—42—1; Holding 19—6—46—2; Croft 19—1—65—3; Garner 16.2—6—39—2; Richards 17—6—24—2.

* captain + wicket-keeper *West Indies won by 298 runs*

13 CHRIS OLD (YORKSHIRE & ENGLAND)

England *v.* Leeward Islands
21–24 March, Monserrat

Chris Old describes the match against the Leeward Islands which was England's second first class victory of the tour. He tells of his surprise at some of the umpires' decisions and goes on to tell of his disappointment when injury ruled him out of the final Test.

At the age of thirty-two I have got to face the fact that my touring days with England must be numbered in my particular cricketing trade — bowling fast medium. This one could possibly have been my last. And if that proves to be the case, it will have been an unhappy one to finish on. I have enjoyed touring and being part of the England set up. The six others I have done — including a previous one to the West Indies under Mike Denness in 1974 — have been among my cricketing highlights. Unfortunately I can't say the same about the last three months in the Caribbean.

The rain, the Guyana situation, Ken Barrington's death and suffering defeats in the first two Test matches played which meant that the series had gone, were not the right ingredients to make it go with a bang generally. Personally I had nothing to lift me either finishing with just five first class wickets and 13 first class runs to my name when I managed to get a game or two in between injuries.

I suppose I should be thankful for the match against the Leeward Islands in Montserrat which brought me three of those wickets and almost a third of those runs. Yet that game was marred by a certain amount of ill feeling caused largely by some umpiring decisions which disturbed us, mutterings from the Leeward Islands captain Vance Amory and a less than amusing performance from their wicket-keeper Shirlon Williams.

It was a great pity. Coming between the Test matches in

Barbados and Antigua it should have been a game in which we could have relaxed instead of finding ourselves getting worked up. The setting was ideal too, a very attractive ground on the outskirts of the capital, Plymouth, with the sea lapping the beach just beyond the boundary at one side and a volcanic mountain range rising up from the other. I cannot recall playing on another first class ground where you could hear the waves crashing on the black sand and rocks.

I was grateful to be playing. A damaged shoulder received when I stretched myself after waking up one morning in Guyana had worried me and I had played one only limited over match against Barbados in the previous month. I'd almost forgotten what it was like to bowl in the middle and whether I could still bowl a line or length.

After all that I was looking forward to bowling on that wicket too. From our hotel balcony we could see the ground and when they took the covers off early on the first morning, it was almost impossible to tell the wicket from the rest of the square. It all looked the same from that distance some half a mile away — one large area of grass. Geoff Miller, leading England for the first time in Ian Botham's absence, had no alternative but to put them in when he won the toss after rain had delayed the start.

It was strange because the ball did very little — except travel to the boundary after a vicious opening assault by their number one batsman Luther Kelly from the island of St Kitts. We learned afterwards that he has taken on all-comers during his couple of seasons playing for the Combined Islands in the Shell Shield competition, quite prepared to hook cheerfully at Michael Holding and company and with a fair degree of success. I think we helped him at the start, being carried away by the grass on the wicket and trying to bowl a little too fast in the hope that the ball would do something.

Despite that I was quite impressed with him. He tucked into Graham Dilley in particular and he and Amory were into three figures in almost even time with Kelly having scored almost two thirds of the runs. He hit Graham Stevenson once which I thought was a certain catch when I watched him connect and smash it in the air. But it kept going up and up and further away over the mid wicket boundary and almost into the sea. It was a prodigous six.

I was thankful he didn't have a go at me when I shared the new ball. Despite my worries I found my line and length immediately as I had done right at the start of the tour in Trinidad. It was pleasing especially when Geoff Miller said to me 'I bet if we put you on in your sleep you would bowl line and length from the first ball.' Not that it did me any good wicketwise in that innings. I bowled five overs at the start for 18 runs and never got another chance to get back on. Once Stevenson had made the breakthrough by dismissing Amory in his second spell, the Leeward Islands side revealed very little in batting strength without Viv Richards who had withdrawn from the game because he was getting married in Antigua.

Having taken 182 not out against us in Barbados, Viv's absence did not distress us too much. Neither did that of Andy Roberts who had also withdrawn to attend the wedding. But it was a shame for the local supporters. It is not often that a touring team drops by the island, not often that they get a chance to see Viv or Andy in action. They had made a great effort to make sure everything was in order for one of the biggest occasions in the island's cricketing history only to find the two stars missing. The crowd was missing as well, boycotting the game because Viv was absent.

By the end of that rain shortened first day Stevenson had taken three wickets and Dilley two. With that success behind them, Geoff Miller naturally gave them another chance on the second morning. They didn't waste it. This time Dilley took three to Stevenson's two and they shared the 10 wickets equally in the Leeward Island innings of 161.

At one time it seemed we would not even match that despite an all Yorkshire 110 run second innings stand between Geoff Boycott and Bill Athey who was playing his first game of the tour since flying in from Australia. We had lost Paul Downton in the third over but Boycott could see his first century of the tour coming up and Athey settled down well particularly against the pace bowlers. Athey struggled a little against the spinners when they first came on, resisting his temptation to hit out against them in order to play a long innings. Neither looked in any particular trouble but suddenly we found ourselves 154 for seven.

After being pinned down on 37 for almost forty minutes by the spinners, Athey was out when the quick bowlers came back for a second burst, caught in the gully off a backfoot forcing shot. Back came off spinner Noel Guishard to have Mike Gatting caught at short leg, bowl Roland Butcher who played down the wrong line. Then came Boycott's personal misfortune when he was on 72. He tried to get in a second run when Geoff Miller played a ball wide of mid-on but was just beaten by an accurate return from local boy Everton Ryan who had been brought into the side to give it extra crowd appeal in Richard's absence but whose ability to wield a bat was summed up by his pair.

With David Bairstow and Graham Stevenson both falling cheaply — there were five Yorkshiremen in the team — we had to rely on a fine innings from Geoff Miller to dig us out of trouble.

I don't think I have seen Geoff Miller bat better. He did well as a captain too. He organised things in the dressing room, talked to the bowlers on the field, willing to give them their head but then insisting on changes if it wasn't working out. He deserved a century for his determination in that innings but seems fated not to get one. Robin Jackman gave him the opportunity by holding up one end for almost two hours and scoring 17 runs out of their 68 run eighth wicket partnership before he was bowled. Unfortunately I managed only four in a short stay and Geoff was nine runs short of his 'ton' when Graham Dilley was caught behind. It's the seventh time in his career that Geoff has been within a few runs of scoring that elusive first century in first class cricket. Three times he has been out in the nineties and four times he has been left not out in the nineties when the last wicket has fallen. We all felt sorry for him.

Thanks mainly to Geoff Miller, we had established a 90 run lead before lunch on the third day. That was the day when the match started to turn a little sour partly as a result of umpiring decisions. I was convinced — along with wicket-keeper Paul Downton and all the close in fielders — that I had their captain Amory caught behind when he was 13 but he was given not out and went on to make 56.

We were all convinced that we had wicket-keeper Shirlon Williams caught three times but he survived each appeal, celebrating each time by smashing the next ball to the boundary. We reminded him that batsmen should get their head down whenever they start a new innings! He had scored 62 by the time Graham Dilley made any appeal unnecessary by clean bowling him.

I'm not blaming the umpires. This was a very big occasion for them which brings extra pressures nobody can understand unless they have stood in the middle themselves. Anybody can make a genuine error; we all do. What saddened me was the attitude of some of the Leeward Island players. Throughout the match Amory, their captain, kept muttering and talking while we were batting. We could hear him clearly fielding, as he did, either in the slips or short leg. If the captain sets that example, other players in the side will soon follow. Once it went unchecked, it spread and in our second innings they appealed for everything. Not just appealing but running towards the umpires gesturing and putting them under pressure. Once Williams even ran to the square leg umpire and put his arms around him when asking for a run out.

If we had responded in a similar way, it might have got out of hand but Geoff Miller quickly and firmly established control when we did allow our annoyance to show. Yet it did take the edge off our performance a little, allowing the Leeward Islands to make 263 in their second innings, setting us a target of 174 to win in five and a half hours.

We were in danger of not getting that at one stage when we found ourselves 73 for four and then 109 for five and the Island players launching into appeals almost everytime the ball beat the bat. Of those first 73, Athey had made 37 with another sound innings before being caught at short leg while Boycott had been given out leg before padding up, a decision he found hard to believe. Fortunately for us, Roland Butcher put an end to all the nonsense in quick time with an unbeaten 77 for his highest score of the tour. We still had five wickets to spare when he hit the winning run to give us our second first class victory of the tour.

Although I couldn't get my run up right and suffered through over stepping which resulted in me being no balled, a trouble I seldom have at home, I managed to pick up three wickets in the Leeward Islands second innings. They were to be my last of the tour.

I had been fit for the Test matches in Barbados and Antigua but had not made the side. That left the last Test in Jamaica as my target. I never made it, ruled out through injury. Because of injuries I've not had the best of luck on recent tours. I just couldn't believe it when a muscle went in the four day match against Jamaica immediately before the final Test. Sharing the new ball with Ian Botham, I had bowled fifteen deliveries without trouble. Then, as I ran in for the sixteenth, I felt a muscle go at the top of my right thigh. I just couldn't believe it was happening to me. Once before I had felt a twang like the one I felt then when tearing a hamstring in rugby practice as a teenager. I bowled two more overs in that spell, had treatment over lunch and bowled another over immediately afterwards but it was no good.

I knew it was fairly serious, kept hoping it wasn't. But when I saw how the top of my thigh had swollen overnight and the expression on the face of Bernard Thomas, our physiotherapist, when he looked at it, I knew my tour was over with more than a week to go.

No, I'm afraid the 1981 tour of the Caribbean is one that never got off the ground on or off the field as far as I was concerned.

LEEWARD ISLANDS v. ENGLAND (4 days)
MONTSERRAT, MARCH 21–24

Leeward Islands

L. Kelly	c Old b Stevenson	72	c Downton b Old	17
*V. Amory	c Gatting b Stevenson	37	b Miller	56
E. Lewis	c Downton b Dilley	1	lbw b Miller	36
+S. Williams	b Stevenson	5	b Dilley	62
E. Ryan	b Dilley	0	lbw b Jackman	0
D. R. Parry	c Butcher b Dilley	1	c Miller b Old	21
J. Archibald	c Downton b Stevenson	7	lbw b Dilley	2
N. Guishard	not out	8	not out	42
A. White	c Bairstow b Stevenson	18	c and b Old	4
J. Harris	c Old b Dilley	0	b Miller	5
V. Newton	b Dilley	0	c Downton b Dilley	6
Extras	b 2, lb 4, nb 6	12	lb 6, nb 6	12
Total		161		263

Fall of wickets: 1—102, 2—111, 3—124, 4—125, 5—128, 6—135, 7—138, 8—157, 9—161.
1—35, 2—106, 3—123, 4—124, 5—190, 6—198, 7—202, 8—216, 9—235

Bowling — first innings: Dilley 13.4—2—48—5; Old 5—2—18—0; Jackman 5—0—22—0; Stevenson 15—5—50—5; Miller 2—0—11—0.
second innings: Dilley 16—5—50—3; Old 18—3—60—3; Stevenson 11—1—64—0; Miller 12—1—42—3; Jackman 12—2—35—1.

England

G. Boycott	run out	72	lbw b Guishard	15
+P. R. Downton	c Williams b Harris	0	c Guishard b Ryan	9
C. W. J. Athey	c Parry b White	41	c Kelly b Parry	37
M. W. Gatting	c Archibald b Guishard	4	c Kelly b Guishard	0
R. O. Butcher	b Guishard	5	not out	77
*G. Miller	not out	91	lbw b Newton	14
D. L. Bairstow	c Amory b Harris	0	not out	14
G. B. Stevenson	b Guishard	3		
R. D. Jackman	b White	17		
C. M. Old	b Harris	4		
G. R. Dilley	c Williams b Guishard	0		
Extras	b 6, lb 3, w 1, nb 4	14	b 5, lb 1, nb 2	8
Total		251	(5 wickets)	174

Fall of wickets: 1—3, 2—113, 3—120, 4—126, 5—128, 6—143, 7—154, 8—222, 9—227.
1—14, 2—45, 3—45, 4—73, 5—109

Bowling — first innings: Harris 23—6—56—3; White 20—6—63—2; Parry 22—6—53—0; Newton 9—2—18—0; Guishard 21.3—5—34—4; Archibald 4—0—13—0.
second innings: Harris 12—3—39—0; White 5—1—16—0; Ryan 6—3—16—1; Parry 14—3—48—1; Guishard 15—4—23—2; Newton 6—1—23—1; Amory 0.1—0—1—0.
England XI won by 5 wickets

14 JOHN EMBUREY (MIDDLESEX & ENGLAND)

Fourth Test

27 March–1 April, Antigua

The fourth Test in Antigua which ended in a draw is described by John Emburey who also tells of his sailing adventures.

Nobody seriously expected us to beat the West Indies when we left England. Nobody had done so since they were able to call upon a four man pace battery to let loose on batsmen the world over and we were a relatively inexperienced side, soon to become even less experienced when we lost Bob Willis and Brian Rose.

Just how much we have to do was clearly visible during the fourth Test match in Antigua when all the conditions helped to even out the strengths of the side down to the food supplied at the ground which brought back memories of home with roast beef, lamb chops and pork chops on the menu instead of the usual diet of fish, rice and peas. A little thing I know, but sometimes these little things mean a lot.

The practice facilities were surprisingly good considering the wicket was pitched in the middle of an open park and must have been trampled on by countless feet every day. The wicket for the Test match was shorn of grass much to the annoyance of Andy Roberts considering it was his home track, the officials were the friendliest we had come across in the West Indies and the hotel was a beauty right beside the sea. And still we came off second best, failed to capitalise on our chances when we had the West Indians head down both with our batting and our bowling. At the end of the drawn match we had to face the unpleasant fact that Clive Lloyd's team had out-thought us all the way along the line. From a personal point of view, I wondered whether I would ever get another Test wicket in the Caribbean not having managed to strike in the Barbados Test either.

In truth we failed in our batting in the first innings which is the one which counts as far as winning is concerned yet twice we were on the verge of making a large score and only scrambled the 271 we did because of a magnificent innings of 102 not out from Peter Willey, the finest I've seen him play and one of the best Test knocks I've seen since I've been watching cricket. And when we had a chance of breaking through with our bowling we were left wanting to allow the last three West Indies wickets put on 172 which meant our only interest in the game over the last couple of days was in trying to rescue ourselves from deep trouble yet again. Fortunately one of those days was lost entirely to the rain which followed us around the Caribbean as if the clouds were attached to us like a balloon on the end of a piece of string.

From my own bowling point of view, I wasn't entirely happy with the team that was chosen. From the moment I'd taken those five wickets in the first Test in Trinidad on a wicket which helped me a little, I had the feeling that all the West Indies batsmen did when they came across me was to try and sit on me, giving me nothing.

With the wicket conditions in Trinidad I was able to bowl a little more slowly, give the ball a little more air but it is asking for a hammering to do that in better conditions against batsmen who were well set. And generally they were well set by the time I came on even when it was early in the innings, given confidence and runs because we often bowled too many loose deliveries at the start which were just sent crashing through the outfield to the boundary.

I felt we desperately needed somebody in our seam attack who could bowl a line and length, restrict the batsmen and make them work for their runs. There was only one in Chris Old, Yorkshire's new captain who is an experienced overseas player although he has the unfortunate habit of breaking down with some niggling injury or other just before a Test match is due.

He would not have played in Guyana if the match had been permitted and missed the Barbados game as well. He was fit for Antigua but was left out which I thought was a mistake. With Robin Jackman also unfit with achilles tendon trouble after using too long spikes on the hard grounds,

Graham Stevenson was brought in for his second Test match. He is probably a more aggressive bowler than Chris but lacks his control as does Ian Botham although he probably produced his best spell of the tour during part of West Indies' first innings.

Two other changes were made and you could not argue with those. Bill Athey stepped in at number three, the only recognised number three in the party and Paul Downton took over again behind the wicket. Roland Butcher had saved his place with his unbeaten 77 in Montserrat although it must still have been a close decision between him and Mike Gatting.

Our practice session on the day before the Test was astonishing. We couldn't use the ground itself because workmen were still putting the finishing touches to a new stand which had been built to celebrate Antigua's first Test, painters and decorators were everywhere and a huge roller was attempting to flatten the outfield.

Instead we were all forced to use an open stretch of parkland just over the road. It was good. For the first time on the tour the local officials had come up with a decent wicket in the most unlikely of circumstances. There was no shortage of spectators either. The West Indies had batted first and no doubt most of them had turned up to watch their idol Viv Richards, the uncrowned king of Antigua, play. They stayed on to watch us too, probably 1,500 at least. There was something in the wicket for the faster bowlers, it took a little spin and it also allowed the batsmen to play their strokes. Just like the Test wicket itself which started to take a little turn towards the end of the third day. I think I might have enjoyed bowling last on it if we had made enough runs to force the West Indies to bat a second time and the rain on the fourth day had not slowed down its deterioration.

For once there was no question of putting the opposition in when Ian won the toss. We had to take first knock and by the end of the first ninety minutes the West Indian heads were beginning to go down. Graham Gooch and Geoff Boycott had 60 runs on the board by then, had seen off the new ball attack without any undue alarms and were ready to grow rich in runs as all batsmen should in those circumstances.

Against an attack like the West Indies I don't suppose any

batsman is ever really in no matter how long he bats. Give them a chance and they are ready to pounce. We gave them that chance in a ridiculous way with Graham running himself out. That was the first setback.

There was no danger at all when Graham smoothly drove Colin Croft straight back towards the sightscreen. It was an easy two but Graham — running towards the danger end — decided to go for a third. He was beaten by a yard. He told us later that Geoff Boycott had actually said 'no' but responded when he decided a third was on. At that stage the fielder Michael Holding had not quite reached the ball. 'If, his return had been a yard wide of the wicket I'd have made it' said Graham. Unfortunately for us Holding covers the ground more quickly than anybody else in their side, he threw on the run and it was just a foot wide when it arrived back with Graham well out of his ground. From 60 without loss we suddenly found ourselves 95 for 3 with Athey and then Boycott following to Croft who had switched to the pavilion end.

With a little bit of help from the West Indies fielders who dropped Roland Butcher twice in his 20, we looked as though we had got over the worst and were still capable of building the type of score we should have done on that wicket when another three wicket clatter ruined us. Roland chanced his arm once too often and was caught at third slip, Ian Botham disappointed me once again with his batting and went to first slip and David Gower was taken at four slip. Three wickets down for the addition of three runs and England 138 for 6.

It meant that England's top batsmen had failed again in the first innings with three of them reaching a stage when they should have been settled and looking for larger things. The captain disappointed me because he had got out in a similar way before on the tour, not quite getting behind the ball and playing it with more of an open face as he would do if he were giving slip catching practice before a day in the field. The West Indies miss very little in the slips with their arc of Lloyd, Richards and Greenidge filling the first three positions.

Peter Willey saved us from complete embarrassment and I was surprised that he had not batted higher up in the order after his performances earlier in the tour when he had shown he could survive only to run out of partners. This time the tail managed to stay with him and I was happy with my contribution which may have been only 10 runs but occupied eighty minutes at the crease while we put on 57 runs for the eighth wicket.

Willey showed us all up by his performance which brought him his second Test century against the West Indies to go with the 100 not out he scored at the Oval in the 1980 summer. Peter hasn't got a lot of technique but what he has got he utilises to the full, backed up by tremendous character and determination. He got behind the deliveries that mattered, played down the ones that rose around chest high, ignored the ones that rose even more and lashed the loose ball to the boundary with the tremendous strength he possesses. He was left on 91 by the close of play with Graham Dilley, our last man, as his partner. Graham did well the second morning to stay with him to allow him to reach a richly deserved century. It was made out of 131 added while he was at the wicket and included fifteen fours plus one astonishing six square of the wicket on the offside against Croft.

Our 271 all out was at least 100 runs short of what it should have been. Once again Croft had inflicted most of the damage by taking 6 for 74 all from the pavilion end and including two dismissals which must have looked astonishing to anybody watching either at the ground or on television. I was the first of those dismissals.

On our first visit to Antigua at the start of the tour manager Alan Smith and the other selectors had noticed that the sight-screen at the popular end of the ground looked very small. They asked for it to be increased in height to cover Joel Garner's arm which would otherwise have come out of a row of trees immediately behind the ground. At Lord's Garner has caused batsmen problems because his arm in delivery is higher than the sightscreen at the Nursery End and the ball is lost in the trees. The Antiguan authorities had complied with our request and increased the height of one sightscreen by more than three feet. What had been overlooked was the narrowness of the sightscreen at the pavilion end. When Croft switched to that end in the Test we found that he was bowling from at least three feet outside the screen because of his wide use of the crease. He was most difficult to pick up and David Gower was hit on the helmet soon after he went in by a Croft bouncer which he did not see.

When I stayed around for a while with Peter Willey it was the signal for Croft to let me have a few short deliveries in an attempt to unsettle me and bounce me out. He did in the end even though the ball which got me was a full toss and hit the wicket about eight inches up from the ground. He was letting me have two and sometimes three short balls an over, most of them difficult to spot because his arm was lost in the crowd. I never really saw the delivery which got me. Partly because I was concentrating on his length in an attempt to avoid being hit by the short ball and not watching the ball all the way from his arm. I was not the only one. Graham Stevenson was 'done' by another full toss soon after, turning his back to avoid being hit when he lost sight of the delivery completely.

The point I made earlier about us not bowling tight enough at the start of a West Indies innings was emphasised that second morning when they started their reply. Desmond Haynes didn't last long before he was brilliantly caught by Paul Downton when he edged an outswinger from the captain. But he lashed a four before he went. Gordon Greenidge's first three scoring shots were boundaries and Viv Richards opened with five in succession.

Fortunately Viv remembered where he was and what the occasion meant to him. Largely through his batting exploits around the world and those of Andy Roberts, the Test match had been granted to Antigua. He has not often been able to reward his most loyal and faithful followers with large, important innings because the Combined Islands, the side he led to the domestic Shell Shield title for the first time in 1981, play only the occasional home match in Antigua. He was determined to make this occasion count especially being watched by his wife of only five days, a wedding that was the social occasion of the year on the island.

Forty-six of his first 50 runs came in boundaries but then he settled down for the century he was after and spent almost three and a half hours over his next 50 runs to reach three figures just before the close when the West Indies were 235 for 2. That left them only 36 runs behind with eight wickets left and Richards ready to cut loose on the third morning in celebration. He was out in the first over having added only another 4 to his overnight 110. He had not accounted for the new ball.

Graham Dilley took it straight away on that third morning and we fancied getting Viv out. He has that touch of arrogance all great batsmen need. There isn't a loose ball he doesn't fancy smashing out of the ground. Graham fed him one just as he had at Berbice in the one day international and at Barbados. It worked again this time. He had already driven Graham for one four when Graham slipped him a shortish one just outside the off stump, one that bounced a little. As soon as he saw the length Viv went for the hook, was surprised a little by the bounce and was not inside it enough when he top edged a simple catch to me at mid-on. I wouldn't have forgiven myself if I had dropped that one especially after all the scheming that had gone on; neither would Graham Dilley.

It was the start of a mini collapse which saw Botham pick up three wickets in five balls in dismissing Everton Mattis who played a poor stroke to cover, Larry Gomes who flicked outside the off stump as David Gower used to do before this tour and David Murray top edging an attempted pull. They were only level with us then and we felt that if we could finish off the innings quickly we could still be in the driving seat especially as the West Indies would have to bat last on a wicket taking a little spin. They don't like being put under pressure. I would always fancy our chances in those situations. We never had the chance.

Once again Clive Lloyd stepped in to lift his side as he had done in Barbados when they had been 65 for 4 in their first innings. He had stopped the rot then by taking the attack to us, driving powerfully, cutting with great precision. He wasn't in the same mood in Antigua. He couldn't time the ball properly at first but his concentration did not waver and he was quite content to rebuild the West Indies position by pushing runs whenever he could.

They were still only 23 ahead when Andy Roberts was bowled by Graham Stevenson but then everything went against us including our own fielding as the last three wickets put on 172 runs. By the time Lloyd was caught behind, the West Indies lead had stretched to 108 runs, Garner having helped him put on 83 for the eighth wicket. Garner made 46 although he might have been out when he had scored five when he attempted to hit me over the top. It was an awkward catch for Graham Stevenson to take and he never looked like finding the right position under the skier.

The last wicket put on 67 before Lloyd declared with Michael Holding and Colin Croft still unbeaten. It should never have grown to that proportion. Croft had made only two when he offered a chance to backward short leg against me but Geoff Boycott was a little slow in reacting. It astonished me that Geoff was even in that position when we had Bill Athey and David Gower on the field. Boycott has a safe pair of hands and catches the ball well in close catching practices but that is different from being in the position all day waiting for just the one chance to come your way. Boycott is one of the best outfielders in the side with a good arm but not a specialist close fielder.

With our pace attack lacking the penetration of the West Indies and the control, there was not much we could have done to have stopped the onslaught. It has been suggested that I should have been used more or Peter Willey who has proved a tight bowler in one day cricket when the slog has been on. I was given two overs but I didn't think I should have been. I was even more convinced when Holding hit me for two sixes, the first beautifully picked off a loose ball which strayed down the leg side, the second a wild slog against a good length ball which just happened to connect. I like bowling against batsmen looking for quick runs when I can bowl to my field and make them take risks in playing orthodox strokes. Against tail enders just slogging for the sake of it, a good, tight faster bowler is in my opinion the man to use.

The runs from Garner, Holding and Croft meant that we were once again left with a rest day in the Test wondering whether we could avoid defeat for the third successive time in the series. Victory was out of the question no matter how well we batted in the second innings. Even if we did not lose wickets we were never going to score fast enough to make up the 197 run deficit and set the West Indians a target. A two day survival exercise was our only hope, two days cut to one when three storms washed out any hope of play on the fourth day.

I was glad to see that rain and not only because it lessened our chances of defeat. On the rest day Mike Gatting and I decided to go sailing. Originally we were going to share a small sailing dinghy but decided it would be more fun to take one each. The wind was quite strong, stronger than I realised when I had travelled out some distance and attempted to turn back to shore. I was experienced enough to use the wind to get me back in again. It was as much as I could do to hold the bow into the waves which were three or four feet high and hope that somebody would spot my trouble.

Mike had got back safely but I was stranded almost half a mile off shore, too far for me to swim in. It got to the point where I was beginning to get frightened. I kept thinking the worst, wondering what would happen if the waves overturned the rather skimpy craft. Fortunately Mike and others on the shore had noticed I was in trouble and a glass bottomed boat used for taking tourists to the coral reef came to my aid, another man climbing on board to help me. Even then it took half an hour to get back.

Defeat still threatened us on that last day especially if we had lost an early wicket or two. Instead we had only one minor scare after Graham Gooch and Geoff Boycott opened with a 144 run partnership, easily the best of the series and almost the best of the tour. Both of them had played superbly before lunch to make sure there was no early breakthrough. Then Graham got carried away a little as he often does when he gets a spinner in his sights. This time it was Viv Richards. He had hit only two boundaries in his first 50 when playing with extreme caution. He hit six more in his next 33 runs, mostly against Viv until he drove a catch to mid-on, an ugly stroke. He should have had his third Test hundred on that last day instead of finishing 17 runs short, missing out again largely because of his own impetuosity.

We were still 53 runs behind at that stage with just over three hours left. Danger threatened when Bill Athey failed again two runs later but Boycott was left behind to go after the century he had set his heart on while David Gower stayed with him long enough for the West Indies to have lost all interest. Boycott likes nothing better than to be able to bat all day in situations where runs are also a secondary consideration. It was a thoroughly professional performance, the type you have come to expect from him over the years but he almost missed out on his twentieth century in Tests. He still needed 11 on 89 with less than two overs left but was helped by a Malcolm Marshall attempt at a run out which brought four overthrows, five runs in all to Geoff off a gentle push worth just one. More importantly from Geoff's viewpoint, it also gave him the strike so that he could complete his 'ton'. During the match Boycott also passed the Test aggregate of Walter Hammond who made 7,249 runs and now only Colin Cowdrey stands ahead of him as the highest scoring England batsman in the history of cricket.

With those two catches going against me towards the tail end of the West Indies first innings I had again finished without a victim but I was still happy with the way I had bowled even though a couple of things were against me. In order to give our faster bowlers as long as possible to recover in between overs in the hot, demanding conditions, I was asked to take my time in bowling my overs which doesn't suit me. Once the ball has been returned to me I like to get back to my mark, turn and go straight in again. In the Caribbean I was always having to fiddle around to eat up valuable seconds.

I wasn't happy either about being told to bowl to Clive Lloyd just outside his off stump in the hope that he would get an edge when he attempted to drive. That was a useful tactic in Trinidad where I was able to turn the ball away from the left hander and any attempted drive carried an element of risk. But it is not the line I like to bowl on a good wicket as Clive demonstrated in Barbados. All it did was to give him extra width allowing him to cut the ball with almost perfect safety which he did on numerous occasions during his first innings 100. Every time he did that and I bowled the next ball on the line I wanted and directed at his stumps, Ian would signal me to bowl wide of the off stump again.

There was one other item I wasn't too happy about either

on the tour, the question of team talks. We had several and each time I thought we spent far too much time talking about the West Indies fast bowlers, how they would bowl, where they would bowl and the rest. We went over it repeatedly and I think it would have been far more beneficial if we had talked about our own problems with the bat and ball and how best we might overcome them instead of worrying about the opposition all the time. I've heard enough about this West Indies side now to last me a lifetime.

WEST INDIES *v.* ENGLAND (fourth Test)
ANTIGUA, MARCH 27–APRIL 1

England				
G. A. Gooch	run out	33	c Greenidge b Richards	83
G. Boycott	c Murray b Croft	38	not out	104
C. W. J. Athey	c Lloyd b Croft	2	c Richards b Croft	1
D. I. Gower	c Mattis b Holding	32	c Murray b Croft	22
R. O. Butcher	c Greenidge b Croft	20		
*I. T. Botham	c Lloyd b Croft	1		
P. Willey	not out	102	not out	1
+P. R. Downton	c Murray b Garner	13		
J. E. Emburey	b Croft	10		
G. B. Stevenson	b Croft	1		
G. R. Dilley	b Murray b Holding	2		
Extras	b 6, lb 7, w 1, nb 3	17	b 11, lb 3, nb 9	23
Total		271		234

Fall of wickets: 1—60, 2—70, 3—95, 4—135, 5—138, 6—138, 7—176, 8—233, 9—233. 1—144, 2—146, 3—217, 8—233, 9—235

Bowling — first innings: Roberts 22—4—59—0; Holding 18.2—4—51—2; Garner 16—5—44—1; Croft 25—5—74—6; Richards 9—4—26—0. second innings: Roberts 17—5—39—0; Holding 9—2—21—0; Garner 15—3—33—0; Croft 16—4—39—2; Richards 22—7—54—1; Gomes 13—5—21—0; Mattis 1—0—4—0.

West Indies		
C. G. Greenidge	c Athey b Stevenson	63
D. L. Haynes	c Downton b Botham	4
I. V. A. Richards	c Emburey b Dilley	114
E. H. Mattis	c Butcher b Botham	71
H. A. Gomes	c Gower b Botham	12
*C. H. Lloyd	c Downton b Stevenson	58
+D. A. Murray	c Boycott b Botham	1
A. M. E. Roberts	b Stevenson	13
J. Garner	c Butcher b Dilley	46
M. E. Holding	not out	58
C. E. H. Croft	not out	17
Extras	b 1, lb 7, w 1, nb 2	11
Total	(9 wickets dec.)	468

Fall of wickets: 1—12, 2—133, 3—241, 4—268, 5—269, 6—271, 7—296, 8—379, 9—401.

Bowling — Dilley 25—5—99—2; Botham 37—6—127—4; Stevenson 33—5- 111—3; Emburey 34—12—84—0; Willey 21—7—31—0; Gooch 2—2—0—0; Boycott 3—2—5—0.

* captain + wicket-keeper

Match drawn

15 GRAHAM DILLEY (KENT & ENGLAND)

The young fast bowler Graham Dilley, who had been ill before the start of the tour and who had only had six weeks practice, describes the conditions and problems of bowling in the West Indies.

No bowler likes being hit for six. Not even a spin bowler who has to suffer a few now and again in plying his particular trade. When it happens to me I feel sick. Even when the batsman is someone like Viv Richards who can deal out sixes against the best bowlers in the world with the merest flick of the wrist and perfect timing.

I felt sick in the third Test in Barbados in the West Indies second innings when Viv sent one delivery from me soaring over the stand at mid wicket and out of the ground. Yet the moment that followed will remain one of my everlasting memories of the Caribbean tour.

Against the previous delivery of fuller length Viv had played a superb shot off his legs during his second innings undefeated 182 which helped set up West Indies' 298 run victory. It looked a four all the way until John Emburey threw himself full length at square leg and made a stop to match the stroke. Viv was clearly annoyed.

I think he made up his mind then that he was going to make the next ball count. It was a little shorter. It seemed that I had no sooner released it than it was soaring over the stand much to the delight of the West Indians in the crowd shouting their approval. My comment wasn't so polite or for the ears of anybody such was my dismay.

Yet I immediately felt much better when Viv walked up the wicket while the car park was being searched for the missing ball. He said to me quietly 'I've wanted to do that to you for a long time'. It wasn't meant nastily. It was a compliment. A signal from the best batsman in the world that I had troubled him, that he had not been able to handle me or take me apart as he had wanted. A mark of progress I had made as a bowler since being tossed into Test cricket only fifteen months earlier against the Australians in Perth on my first England tour.

In fact my duels with Viv became quite a feature of the tour. With his liking for trying to dominate the bowling from the start it was felt that my extra pace might prove his undoing if I could tempt him into error. Generally I managed to come out on top which helped to make up for all my other disappointments.

Including the second one day international in Berbice, Guyana, Viv played six innings against us on the tour. He was not out in that second innings in Barbados. He was caught off Geoff Miller in his only innings in Trinidad. And he fell to me on the other four occasions, three times not getting into position to play the stroke he wanted but arrogantly going through with the shot.

In Berbice, the first time I had a chance of getting at Viv on the tour, I fed him a shortish ball just outside his off stump which he attempted to hook only to send it many a mile in the air for Graham Stevenson to take the catch on the long leg boundary. He made only three that day.

In the first innings in Barbados he was out for a duck, attempting to drive the first ball he faced from me but was beaten by the bounce for Ian Botham to take a fine catch high to his left at second slip. Moving on to Antigua another attempted hook brought his downfall.

He had made his century by then on his home ground in the first Test Antigua had staged. He came out on the third morning to put the icing on the cake, ready to take us all apart despite the fact we had taken the new ball first thing. The first ball he faced from me he turned to square leg for four. It was well pitched up. So were the next two which he blocked. Then I slipped him the short one outside the off stump. He was never in line to play the hook shot. He was also beaten by the bounce. But he still went through with the stroke only to give John Emburey an easy catch at mid-on. He was mine again, just as he was in Jamaica when he was caught behind attempting a leg glance.

Despite getting Viv four times out of six I still left the Caribbean disappointed with the number of Test wickets I picked up — only 10 in all at a cost of 45 runs each. It was tough; tougher than I expected. Tougher than it had been in Australia on my first tour or at home during the 1980 summer against them. I only hope I have learned from the experience and get a chance to play against Australia this summer so that I can have another chat with Dennis Lillee to find out exactly where I go from here to make myself the bowler I want to be. He has helped me tremendously with his words of advice.

I found the going tough in the Caribbean for two main reasons. There is less margin for error against batsmen who have, in the main, been brought up on a diet of fast bowling on wickets which provide little lateral movement. Stray just a little in length or line and they give it the 'wellie' with all their might. I also missed a new ball partner with the ability to keep the batsmen under control once Bob Willis was forced home and Chris Old forced out of the Test reckoning with a series of injuries. I was left wondering how successful their four fast bowlers would have been if they had been forced to operate as an individual instead of part of a complete machine.

Losing Bob Willis was my biggest blow. Not only as a new ball partner but as somebody I could have turned to for advice. With all his experience of overseas wickets he knows exactly what to bowl and where to bowl. He is also one person who is prepared to hand over that advice to a youngster, sit and talk things over with you. Without him to fall back on, I was torn between listening to some who advised me to bowl as fast as I could in the hope of roughing up their batsmen and those who said that I should have concentrated more on line and length even at the expense of a little pace.

It was also easier bowling against the West Indies at home during the 1980 summer when I had either Chris Old or Mike Hendrick operating at the other end with the new ball. Both bowl such a tight, mean length, neither gives the batsmen a chance to get away to a flying start. It is such a tremendous help knowing you can take an extra risk in attacking the batsmen secure in the knowledge runs will not be flowing from the other end.

Ian Botham will be the first to admit he is not that type of bowler. He likes to attack, loves to experiment and consequently, bowls a number of loose deliveries mixed in with his good ones. As I said earlier, anthing loose in the Caribbean against Gordon Greenidge and Desmond Haynes is asking for trouble. I wonder what might have happened if we had taken a chance and given Robin Jackman the new ball in one innings. Like Chris Old and Mike Hendrick, he bowls a strict line and length and was never collared in the two Tests he played despite his lack of pace.

The constant breaks during the early part of the tour did not help either. I never felt I struck my true rhythm after Trinidad when the rain in Guyana followed by the political fuss over Robin Jackman's arrival meant that we went a fortnight without any serious cricket.

Until then I had bowled regularly. A good outing in the first match against the Young West Indies side in Pointe-a-Pierre when I soon discovered in my first spell it was necessary to change from an English approach. With very little movement off the wicket and only variable bounce to help, you can't expect to take wickets with the type of deliveries which succeed in England. After that opening spell, Ken Barrington was after me to bowl line and length, forcing the batsmen to take the chances if they wanted to score.

In the island match against Trinidad and the first Test in Port of Spain I was very happy with the way I bowled — except that I was not rewarded with wickets. In the West Indies innings I bowled 28 overs which cost only 73 runs, beat the bat on numerous occasions even when Greenidge and Haynes rushed away to a 168 start. Yet, at the end of it, I had nothing to show for my performance in terms of wickets. It was all very well for everybody to come along and congratulate me on my bowling but there is only one thing which keeps me going — a few victims to show for it. When their innings was finally over I must confess that I just grabbed a drink and went away from everybody, finding a quiet corner where I could sit alone. I didn't feel like talking.

A number of people commented that I would bowl less well and finish up with a hatful. I didn't believe them at the time. But it worked out that way when I took five for 45 in 13.4 overs in the Leeward Islands first innings in Montserrat halfway through the tour. I'll be the first to admit I bowled rubbish in that innings. Those five wickets improved my overall tour figures but they don't compensate for missing out against Test batsmen when I felt in the groove.

As far as my Test figures were concerned, my four wickets in the final Test match in Kingston, Jamaica were a tremendous boost. Even then it might have been better but for boot trouble. On the second morning when the West Indies started their first innings, the wicket was playing faster than it had on the first day.

I know I surprised Gordon Greenidge with two deliveries in my first over. The third delivery beat him completely, went right through him. The last one bounced more than he expected as he went to hook, found his glove and went just over the hands of wicket-keeper Paul Downton for a one bounced four to the sightscreen. Either might have brought his wicket.

At the end of that over I thought it might be my day. But halfway through my fourth over I lost the heel on my right boot and was forced off the field. The bootmaker who had been around earlier in the day was missing and by the time the rest of the England players had carried out an emergency repair and I could start bowling again, the new ball had lost its shine and was already looking soft and tattered.

That was another disappointment but there were compensations. My biggest worry when the tour started was how my strength would hold up after my attack of glandular fever the previous August which put me out of the season at home and stopped me doing any serious training until six weeks before the Caribbean tour began.

Fortunately it was not a problem. Physically I felt good throughout the three months, desperately tired at times but able to come through fairly long spells in strength sapping conditions and still come back fairly sharp late in the day. The only serious injury I encountered had nothing to do with the strain of bowling but a yorker from Joel Garner in Berbice which caught me on the big toe of my right foot causing a hairline fracture and a swelling which prevented me getting on my bowling boots for a week. That injury apart I came through the tour unscathed which is saying something as far as fast bowlers are concerned these days.

I would like to finish on one small plea to batsmen on the tour. To ask them to remember that fast bowlers need to get in net practice as much as they do when there is so little first class cricket around in between the Test matches. Twice on the tour I was banished from the nets because I was bowling too fast and presented an injury risk which I thought was unfair.

I admit the net facilities were not good on either occasion. All the more reason, I would have thought, for the batsmen to kit themselves out properly with thigh pads, chest protectors and crash helmets as they would in the middle to get a taste of what they could expect when they came across the West Indies pace attack. It's a point to bear in mind for the future.

16 MIKE GATTING (MIDDLESEX & ENGLAND)

England *v.* Jamaica
4–7 April

The match against Jamaica is seen through the eyes of Mike Gatting who had a disappointing start to the tour but who made a comeback in this match. He tells of the two young Jamaican spin bowlers, Tucker and Malcolm, and of the problems they caused him.

None of us was looking forward to Jamaica. It was a rather apprehensive bunch of England cricketers who stepped off the aircraft at Norman Manley Airport in Kingston for the last leg of the tour wondering what was going to happen next. Following Robin Jackman's deportation from Guyana it was always felt that Jamaica might prove the next problem country and we arrived in the knowledge that there had been a renewed call to ban Robin from entry.

The uneasy feeling wasn't helped when we were all whisked through customs and immigration with almost indecent haste only to be met outside by a strong cordon of policemen equipped with a variety of weapons including M16 rifles, Sterling sub machine guns and Smith and Wesson revolvers. They were everywhere, providing an escort for our coach to the hotel with manager Alan Smith riding 'shotgun' in the lead police jeep.

The hotel itself looked more like a prison with so many guards around, including two stationed on the floor of the hotel where we were all accommodated for safety. Every visitor to the floor was checked immediately they left the lifts including manager Alan Smith when he came to visit us on the first night. We had our own special eight man detachment looking after us. Everywhere we went, they came too even when we spent a day on the golf course or went shopping in a city where street gun battles between troublemakers and the police were so commonplace they rated only a paragraph or two in the newspapers.

The Sabina Park ground itself was bristling with almost every type of weapon imaginable as the police called on the Jamaica Defence Force for reinforcements. We had a shock, too, when we first arrived at Sabina Park to find the ambitious rebuilding scheme had been held up through a lack of materials and import controls which left the new, huge concrete stand little more than a shell surrounded by so much rubble it looked more like a builder's yard.

Yet I for one found peace of mind in Jamaica to end what had been an agonising tour personally on a high note even though I failed to get my place back for the final Test. With the massive security cordon thrown around us, we were all able to relax and not once did we encounter the slightest sign of trouble or hostility from a friendly crowd who went out of their way to make us feel welcome.

Our own hand picked guard attachment became almost part of the team so readily did they mix in, conspicuous in the day time when they were in uniform, mixing into the background during the evenings when they changed into plain clothes but always accompanied by their revolvers. Their leader Roland was a giant of a man, protective and courteous while Billy the Kid soon became a favourite. That was not his real name but the one we gave him. He was a left handed gun which he housed in a holster specially made for a quick draw worn cowboy style, low slung and tied down to his left thigh with a leather thong. He was quick too when we put him to the test in the safety of our team room.

I desperately needed those 93 runs I scored in the first innings of the drawn match against Jamaica after what had happened over the previous weeks of the tour when I had been out four times for single figures including two ducks. I needed the second innings 42 to go with them to prove to myself the first innings had not been just a one off situation.

The tour had started so well for me. During the 1980 summer at home I had felt so confident that I walked to the wicket each time almost convinced nobody could get me out. And that is how I felt during the first match against the Young West Indies at Pointe-a-Pierre when making 94 after just over four hours at the wicket. That should have set me up for the entire visit. Instead I hardly managed to make a run after that although I felt I did little wrong.

I must confess that my confidence took a little knock when I wasn't selected for the first Test in Trinidad. I was in the twelve named, David Gower and myself being the only two middle order batsmen who had made runs at that stage but Geoff Miller won the number five batting position when it was decided to go in with three spinners. When I did get my Test chance in the third Test in Barbados it was as an emergency number three batsman following the return home of Brian Rose. That was when my troubles began although I felt I was a little unfortunate to get out to one that shot along the ground in the second innings of the match against Barbados when I had made 22 and was feeling in good form.

It's no crime to get out cheaply. The crime is getting out when you've been at the wicket for an hour of more, played yourself in and fail to make 50 or more. I never had that chance in my next four innings. In the two Test innings I went to the wicket each time before the England innings was two overs old, a little unlucky, I thought, to get a shooter first ball in the second dig.

Having been out four times almost within minutes of getting to the crease in the Test and in the following game against the Leeward Islands in Montserrat and then going without an innings for more than a week when I missed the fourth Test in Antigua, I had no idea what sort of form I was in when my turn came against Jamaica after Ian Botham had won the toss and decided to bat.

I had to wait for some time too after Geoff Boycott and Graham Gooch had put on a 55 run start before Graham went on the charge against off spinner Richard Austin and was stumped. By the time Bill Athey, David Gower and Roland Butcher had been and gone and Geoff was looking set for another century, we had 193 on the board before I walked to the wicket.

It was not a life or death situation but I needed runs for myself if not the side. I also made a conscious decision before I went in that I was not going to wear a crash helmet even though Jamaica fast bowlers Junior Williams and Percy Tomlinson were fairly sharp if not accurate and made the ball bounce. With the helmet offering protection against the pace bowlers, I felt that I had been getting into some bad and false positions, making errors I should not have done. I decided that the only way to rectify the position was to expose myself to an element of physical danger, forcing me to do away with any preconceived ideas of what to do and treat each ball on its merit. If it meant taking hasty evasive action to avoid being hit, I was prepared for that. I felt I needed to bring a little more discipline into my game. You need to be disciplined to make the grade at a Test level.

I almost did not have that chance. The first ball I faced against off spinner Marlon Tucker I attempted to cut against the spin and would have been caught at first slip if Jamaica captain and former West Indies batsman Lawrence Rowe had been a little more alert. Many will argue I should never have attempted that shot against the first delivery I received but it is one that has brought me many runs during my shortish career. They are probably right but I felt extremely nervous when I first went in, thought the shot was on and it's my natural game not to hold back in such circumstances. I'm a boundary seeker by nature but after that escape I became determined to settle down and curb myself. Apart from hitting one spinner back over the top I don't think I really played a shot in anger during my 222 minutes at the areas at the crease. The most pleasing thing about my innings was that in abandoning my natural game I didn't lose my concentration.

Geoff and I put on 85 for the fifth wicket before he was out two short of his second successive century when he was caught at second slip after 294 minutes at the wicket. He had never really been in trouble but both of us needed to be watchful against two young Jamaican spinners, Tucker and Donovan Malcolm, a left armer of high promise. Both are only twenty-one and good enough to suggest that the West Indies could pose problems at a Test level in future years once their battery of fast bowlers starts to creak apart.

Malcolm caused the most trouble especially when he pitched it up a little. Even on the first day he was able to make the ball turn appreciably, made his top spinner bounce in a surprising fashion. He has a nice, high action with a lovely loop but on that particular wicket I didn't think he pushed it through quite quickly enough to force the batsmen to play what I would term 'getting out shots'. On most occasions I found it fairly easy to play him and swept him without too much concern. Of the pair I thought off spinner Tucker was the more dangerous. He did not give the ball so much air but still managed an astonishing degree of turn. He proved a useful batsman too and it was not surprising to learn he led the young West Indies side to England in 1980.

I know Geoff was more impressed with Malcolm, probably because Malcolm claimed his wicket. It was Tucker who got mine when I was seven short of my century — out cutting again only to give a catch behind. We had scored 413 when I was eighth out, our final score.

Jamaica's reply of 368 was built largely around a century by Rowe who still looks one of the most polished and accomplished batsmen in the world although he didn't figure in the West Indies plans against us because of a poorish return in their domestic Shell Shield programme. Not that we were upset by his absence. Some of his strokes through the offside were sheer perfection bringing all but three of his sixteen fours in his four and a half hours at the wicket until he fell leg before to our captain.

He shared in a 102 run partnership with opener Richard Austin for the third wicket and another of 114 with Mark Neita which produced one of the most amusing incidents of the tour. A stocky, hard hitting batsman he annoyed Ian Botham when he edged him three or four times through the slips. Each time Ian increased his number of slips until he had six in a line only to overpitch the next delivery which Neita on drove firmly to the vast, unattended acres beyond.

Immediately he released the ball Ian realised his error. The only fielder in front of the wicket was at extra cover and Ian had not got to the end of his follow through before he was forced to turn and start a seventy yard chase to the boundary, spared the final ten yards of the run when the ball beat him to the line.

Jamaica's first innings task had been made easier by the fact that half way through his opening spell Chris Old tore a muscle high in his right thigh and was forced off the field leaving us short of bowlers — and emergency fielders. Geoff Miller was forced to pull out of the match on the first morning because of an attack of flu, Paul Downton had to retire with a similar attack and Geoff Boycott went to his bed after his innings with a sore throat. With Graham Stevenson nursing a damaged thigh muscle we were even forced to call upon manager Alan Smith as a substitute fielder at one stage.

The bowling shortage meant a long spell for John Emburey, my Middlesex colleague, and he bowled marvellously in taking six for 92 off his thirty-four overs, beating most of the batsmen through the air rather than off the wicket. Amazingly, they were his first wickets since the match against Barbados over a month before yet he had bowled superbly, so well that the batsmen who knew him rarely took a chance against him. The unsuspecting Jamaican batsmen did — and perished.

We were only 45 ahead when we started our second innings on the third evening and there was still a danger that we might be in for an embarrassing defeat on the eve of the final Test when we lost Paul Downton — opening in Boycott's absence — Bill Athey and David Gower increasing our lead by 78. Fortunately Graham Gooch was in the mood to show everybody what a class batsman he has become.

He rather gave it away in the first innings when the spinners first came on. Without Boycott and seeing the early wickets fall, he got his head down in the second although he still never missed an opportunity to belt the ball for six if he thought the stroke was on. But they were all cool, well measured strokes this time in making his third century of the tour, going on to make 122 until he drove off spinner Austin to deep mid-off after almost four hours at the wicket with 14 fours and three sixes.

That let me in again. By that time we were 230 ahead and some people were suggesting that Ian Botham should declare to make a game of it but there was hardly any point. With about three hours left, Jamaica would have been the only side to benefit.

With the Test match ahead Ian was thinking more about our own problems. He wanted to have a longish innings in the middle himself after his own disappointing run of low scores and there was still the final England middle order batting place to settle, a place that rested between Roland Butcher and myself.

I had obviously returned to the reckoning with my 93 in the first innings, Roland having made 44. He was struggling to assert himself in the second innings during his 117 run partnership for the fourth wicket with Graham and was still struggling to make any real headway when I joined him in a 61 run partnership for the next wicket. Of those runs I made 42 and was feeling rather good but still not good enough, as it turned out, to win my Test place back.

Apart from getting on the field as emergency fieldsman during the final Test, that innings turned out to be my last contribution to the tour. Although I had scored my 42 runs in good time, scored with great freedom Roland, as the man in possession, retained his place with a fighting three hour half century, both of us falling to the off spin of Everton Mattis much to the delight of his home crowd. In fact he took the last four wickets, denying Ian Botham his longish innings in the middle although his bowling cannot be taken too seriously. It just went to emphasise what a cruel sport cricket can be at times when an occasional bowler comes on and grabs four for 22 when genuine bowlers with far greater ability are denied wickets even when they have bowled magnificently.

It was disappointing to make the Test side only once — and that in a false position — after the way I had started the tour. Yet the two innings in Jamaica confirmed the feeling I had throughout the three months in the Caribbean — I had never been out of form but denied the chance to show it by the run of early dismissals.

JAMAICA v. ENGLAND
JAMAICA, APRIL 4–7

England

G. A. Gooch	st Dujohn b Austin	31	c A. B. Williams b Austin	122
G. Boycott	c Mattis b Malcolm	98	not out	4
C. W. J. Athey	lbw b J. Williams	11	lbw b Tucker	25
D. I. Gower	run out	24	c Austin b Malcolm	0
R. O. Butcher	c Tomlinson b Tucker	44	st Dujohn b Mattis	51
M. W. Gatting	c Dujohn b Tucker	93	c Dujohn b Mattis	42
*I. T. Botham	c Austin b Tomlinson	26	c Malcolm b Mattis	14
C. M. Old	c Malcolm b Tomlinson	8		
J. E. Emburey	c Austin b Malcolm	34	c and b Mattis	1
R. D. Jackman	not out	0	not out	11
+P. R. Downton	absent ill	0	lbw b J. Williams	0
Extras	b 8, lb 21, w 1, nb 14	44	b 16, lb 4, nb 4	24
Total		413	(8 wickets)	294

Fall of wickets: 1–55, 2–95, 3–134, 4–194, 5–278, 6–312, 7–330, 8–413, 9–413.
1–1, 2–77, 3–78, 4–196, 5–257, 6–264, 7–272, 8–285.

Bowling — first innings: J. Williams 22–2–77–1; Tomlinson 23–5–60–2; Austin 26–2–95–1; Malcolm 28.2–6–77–2; Tucker 21–4–60–2.
second innings: J. Williams 16–7–28–1; Tomlinson 16–2–45–0; Austin 19–2–50–1; Malcolm 20–5–51–1; Tucker 25–4–69–1; Mattis 13.5–6–22–4; Neita 2–2–0–0; A. B. Williams 2–0–5–0.

Jamaica

R. A. Austin	c Butcher b Emburey	62
A. B. Williams	c Gooch b Botham	10
E. H. Mattis	b Jackman	15
*L. G. Rowe	lbw b Botham	116
+J. Dujohn	b Emburey	6
H. S. Chang	run out	12
M. Neita	st Downton b Emburey	67
M. A. Tucker	lbw b Emburey	36
D. Malcolm	c sub b Emburey	6
J. Williams	not out	11
P. Tomlinson	st Downton b Emburey	7
Extras	b 1, lb 3, nb 16	20
Total		368

Fall of wickets: 1–17, 2–39, 3–141, 4–153, 5–181, 6–295, 7–327, 8–335, 9–356

Bowling — Old 6–1–20–0; Botham 23–2–111–2; Emburey 34–9–92–6; Jackman 21–6–57–1; Gooch 16–58–0; Gatting 3–1–10–0.

* captain + wicket-keeper

Match drawn

17 DAVID GOWER (LEICESTERSHIRE & ENGLAND)

Fifth Test
10–15 April, Jamaica

The man who made the highest individual score of the series describes the final Test in Jamaica.

Sitting down on the rest day of the last Test to make notes for this chapter helped me obtain what I needed most from my tour of the Caribbean — the big hundred over the last two days on my final visit to the crease to convince myself, if nobody else, that I had really come to terms with Test cricket at its highest level.

From the moment I had walked away from the wicket after almost eight hours at the crease following my first innings of 187 in the opening match of the tour against the Young West Indies team, I had felt that this was going to be *my* tour.

When I regained my England place for the Centenary Test against Australia at Lord's the previous September I felt I belonged there such was my form at the time. I had finished off the England season on a high note with a century against Hampshire in Leicestershire's final game. That had set me up for the Caribbean where I had arrived refreshed, batteries recharged after a three month break. That first innings in Pointe-a-Pierre had confirmed everything I had felt about the three months ahead.

I had felt good then. I had felt good everytime I walked to the wicket throughout the West Indies. I had felt good at the crease even though the runs were not exactly flowing in the middle of the tour. People watching, my team-mates were kind enough to tell me from time to time that I was looking good. Yet, when I sat down in my hotel room to make the notes covering the first three days of the final Test in Sabina Park, Kingston and how the tour had gone for me personally, I became increasingly conscious that I had not really done justice to myself. I got up the following morning when we were due to start our second innings, determined not to return to the dressing room when my chance came without at least a century against my name.

Perhaps it was a selfish attitude. But people throughout the ages have written that the makers of large centuries have all had a streak of selfishness about them. It was a selfishness inspired too by England's position for we began again after the rest day in the all too familiar position of having to fight to save the match just as we had done in the three previous Tests.

It is almost impossible to describe the feeling of relief which swept over me at the end when I kept out the final delivery from Larry Gomes and was able to walk away with 154 runs to my credit — England's highest individual score of the series, my fourth Test century and certainly the most satisfying even though it did not match the heights, in terms of runs, of my 200 not out against the Indians at Edgbaston in 1979.

The fact that it was England's highest individual total of the series was almost an accident. When the final over started I had scored 153, exactly the same as Graham Gooch's magnificent performance in our first innings and I toyed seriously of sticking on the same total. I even mentioned it to Paul Downton who had stuck solidly and courageously with me during the final three hours but when Larry Gomes bowled me a particularly loose delivery, I couldn't resist hitting it for the single which took me ahead. There are sufficient times in cricket where you don't get one run to turn down a chance when the opportunity was there!

Graham Gooch's first innings 153 had been superb, almost a bonus because we had arrived on the ground that first morning fearing the worst on a wicket which threatened to be the fastest of the tour. The Jamaican fast bowlers had been able to extract a great deal of bounce from the wicket for the island match and we had all been warned that the Test wicket six yards away would be just as bouncy and even faster. We felt too that we would not get any choice about whether to bat first or not, Ian Botham having won the toss in the three previous Tests. Clive Lloyd was certain to win this one.

He did and although he did not make up his mind immediately about whether to put us in, Geoff Boycott had no doubt about what his decision would be. Geoff had already strapped on his chest protector and thigh pad before we were officially informed the honour was ours.

Surprisingly, the wicket did little for either Michael Holding on his home ground or Malcolm Marshall playing his first Test in the West Indies in place of Andy Roberts who had been dropped after failing to take a wicket in the previous Test. Before the first over was completed Holding was looking at the ball with suspicion and the wicket with dismay.

For an hour very little happened except that Geoff and Graham dug themselves in. But it looked a very different match as soon as Colin Croft was brought into the attack with his wide angle of delivery and his ability to get far more bounce out of the wicket than anybody else. We might easily have fallen apart at that stage. Whenever he had come on in the previous Tests he had usually taken a wicket and might have had one then, introducing a note of desperation into Graham's batting after one over when Graham might have been caught at slip, bowled or taken at short leg.

Graham's answer was to take the attack to Croft this time. There was an element of risk about some of his strokes but he continued to hit the ball with such power that even when the ball was in the air, it went through the field to the boundary before the fielders had time to react. Together they put on 95 before Geoff was out soon after lunch, just getting a touch to one from Joel Garner which bounced and moved away. We'd have settled for that start before the match began. Our total would have looked pretty sick without those 95 runs, sicker still without Graham's contribution.

He was in full cry by mid-afternoon. Of the 55 runs added for the second wicket Bill Athey made only three in the 50 minutes he was at the wicket with Graham. He had reached his half century with a six over third man off Croft, a stroke described as 'part steer, part cut, part drive off an ascending delivery which went over second slip and the perimeter of the four boundary line' by one local scribe. He celebrated by hitting Croft for three fours in succession in the next over and, for once, the lanky Guyanese bowler retired from the attack feeling bruised and battered instead of us.

Unfortunately the rest of us found strange ways of getting out instead of staying with him. After fifty minutes Bill Athey, rather unfortunate to be thrown into the deep end after arriving halfway through the tour, was bowled behind his legs. The same thing happened to me just when I thought runs were beginning to flow smoothly and Peter Willey, batting at number five, was taken behind down the leg side flicking at a delivery that had strayed off line. I'd been out the same way in Antigua and I regarded both dismissals as rather unlucky. In both cases we got just the thinnest of touches off loose deliveries which were potential four balls, the West Indies having nobody in a catching position behind square on the leg side.

There is no way, however, I should have been outbowled behind my legs. And that made me stop and think of the ways I had been out in the Test series. Looking back, I thought there was only one genuinely bad shot that had brought about my downfall, the second innings in the third Test in Barbados when I had reached 54 and should have gone on to make a century in a situation where we needed to bat out time to save the game.

Although I say it myself, I had gone well in that innings when joining with Graham Gooch in adding 120 for the third wicket after we had been two for two. Together we had seen off the fast bowlers, forcing Clive Lloyd to turn to Viv Richards and his off spin in an attempt to get the breakthrough he wanted. As soon as Viv came on I told myself 'You musn't get out to him' I did. For more than two and a half hours we had survived the fast bowlers and it is very difficult not to let yourself relax a little when you see a slow bowler come on. The sight of one also brings a different mental approach to the game. Instead of blocking and blocking for hours, intent on survival and smashing the occasional loose delivery, you start thinking of where you are going to score runs. The stroke I played against Viv was a bad one, a black mark. I was just trying to dab it down wide of the wicket-keeper but it kept drifting in. I didn't move my feet to compensate and could only help it on to my off stump in the end. A bad stroke as I said especially as it was going to bring me only one run at the most.

I count myself a little unlucky in two other dismissals, in the first innings at Port of Spain, Trinidad and the first innings in the Barbados match. On both occasions it was raining when I got out and that has to be unfortunate in the Caribbean. On both occasions too I looked back as I walked to the dressing room only to find the rest of the players following me, the umpires having decided that the rain was too heavy for the match to be continued. The rain was no worse then than it had been at the start of the over and my dismissals highlight the problems the umpires face in deciding exactly when conditions are bad enough for play to be interrupted. If I had not got out when I did I wonder whether play would have been stopped at that time. Or what might have happened in those matches if play had been stopped immediately before the over in which I had been out.

I wasn't particularly happy about my dismissals in either case. In Trinidad I had been given out leg before against Colin Croft. He seemed to be able to make the ball talk out in the Caribbean so erratically did it behave when he bowled but I thought it must have been capable of doing some extraordinary things to hit the wicket if my leg had not been in the way even allowing for his angle of delivery. In Barbados I felt I was doubly unfortunate in that Everton Mattis took the catch at fourth slip, the first thing he had held on the tour up until then. Even on that occasion the ball escaped his hands, catching it in his midriff as he doubled up and staying there long enough to get his hands to it.

The only other batsman to stay with Graham for any length of time in Jamaica was Roland Butcher playing what I thought was his best innings of the tour. He was probably a little lucky to still find himself in the side after the innings of 93 and 42 by Mike Gatting in the match against Jamaica. For most of the time he had struggled to make an impression but in that first innings in the final Test his feet looked right, he moved well and got into position quickly to hit some nice, crisp drives through the offside.

He was still there when Graham's innings came to an end after five and a quarter hours at the crease with two sixes and twenty-one fours in his 153. His ending was quite spectacular too, a diving, one handed catch by wicket-keeper David

Murray when Graham got an inside edge driving against Holding. At that stage Graham had made more than half of our 249 for five. The end was not far away.

In dismissing Geoff Boycott in Barbados and forcing Ian Botham to throw away his bat in frustration, Holding had looked remarkably quick in the third Test. On the second morning in Jamaica he was astonishing in taking three for two in 12 deliveries to finish off our first innings. The wicket was much faster than it had been at the start and batsmen in the best of nick would have struggled to have kept him out. Once Ian Botham had fallen in Malcolm Marshall's first over with the new ball, the tail was cruelly exposed.

Paul Downton did well to get the bat under his chin to fend one off against Holding but had no chance of controlling the ball as it flew to backward square leg. John Emburey was completely beaten by sheer pace when he lost his middle stump and Robin Jackman confessed he was 'bruised and bemused' when he returned to the dressing room, lucky not to have had his left hand shattered after twice being struck on the hand. He was in considerable pain.

The bounce and pace Holding had extracted from the wicket at least offered us some hope that Graham Dilley might be able to do the same when the West Indies batted on that second morning and pick up a couple of wickets with the new ball. He bowled two deliveries in the first over which Gordon Greenidge knew little about, one that went right through him and another which went off his gloves and went for a one bounce four just over the outstretched gloves of Paul Downton.

But then we were hit by an unfortunate incident. Half way through his fourth over Graham lost the heel on his right boot and was forced to go off. Amazingly, he did not have a spare pair of solid bowling boots with him which meant that he had to return to the field in an ordinary pair of boots and could not bowl. The incident raised a laugh with the near twenty-thousand crowd, the largest to watch a Test in Jamaica, when an appeal was broadcast over the public address system for a 'boot repairer to report to the England dressing room'. On the field we found little to laugh about however and the experience should have taught Graham to make sure his boots are in perfect working order and to always have a spare pair with him.

By the time Geoff Miller and the other substitute fielders had repaired the heel, the new ball had lost its shine and hardness and Gordon Greenidge and Desmond Haynes were away. Robin Jackman had been forced to take over Graham Dilley's bowling stint but was the first to admit he could not get going in that pre lunch session, his left hand still throbbing from the battering it had received from Holding.

Considering the 116 run start the West Indies had before Dilley had Greenidge caught at second slip, we did well to hold the West Indies that day to 193 for three at the close, still 92 runs behind when the third morning started and the new ball available. Viv Richards looked ready to take us apart when he started with two fours and a six in his 15 runs before being caught down the leg side by Paul Downton flicking at a loose ball in the same way Peter Willey had done. We also dismissed Haynes when he was 16 runs short of the century he had set his heart on getting forcing Clive Lloyd to promote himself one place up the order to give aid and comfort to Everton Mattis who was having a miserable time in his first Test before his home supporters.

Haynes had fallen to Peter Willey whose off spin was having its first lengthy airing of the series. That had been a deliberate decision taken at our team meeting before the start of the final Test. It was felt by some of the more senior players that our bowling changes had not been adventurous enough in previous matches when the West Indian batsmen had settled in. Ian Botham was urged to give Willey more of a go, mix up the bowling a little more in an attempt to present batsmen with more problems instead of settling into a groove. Willey is not the worst off spinner in Test cricket these days and is a greater spinner of the ball than John Emburey although he doesn't use the air so well. Ian accepted the advice given at the team talk and it worked when Haynes was played across the line.

We arrived at the ground on the third morning with our hopes high of being able to put the West Indies under real pressure for the first time in the series if we could make a significant breakthrough with the new ball which was due immediately. We had a chance — and then let it slip when Everton Mattis was put down by Ian Botham at second slip off Graham Dilley. It was a bad miss.

The wicket was still playing faster than on the first morning and Mattis had been disturbed by the previous delivery from Graham which rose steeply, forcing him to jerk his head out of the way at the last moment. Mattis was wearing his West Indies cap at the time, a cap presented to him during the fourth Test in Antigua and one I gathered he had hardly taken off. It fell off that time and he immediately signalled for different headwear. It was assumed he was asking for a crash helmet after being only a fraction of an inch away from being hit but he demanded a floppy sun hat instead, easier to keep on than a cap.

The next delivery from Graham Dilly bounced again catching the edge of Mattis' bat and offering Graham Gooch a straightforward catch chest high at first slip — until Ian made a last minute grab with his left hand and spilled it. I shall long remember the anguished cry of 'Oh Both' from Graham Gooch and the look of complete despair on Graham Dilley's face.

The new ball was less than three overs old at the time, a severe test for new batsmen Larry Gomes if only we could have got at him. By the time that Dilley had Mattis caught off a poor stroke at extra cover, the ball was eight overs old, both Dilley and Botham tired. Our main chance had gone with Clive Lloyd and Gomes adding 118 for the fifth wicket in taking the West Indies ahead and putting us under pressure once again.

Clive's batting had been one of the highlights of the tour as far as the West Indies were concerned, making runs every time he went to the wicket including the century in Barbados when his side were 64 for four. He played then as if he had not a care in the world, enjoying the new lease of Test life a successful knee operation in Australia fifteen months earlier has given him. He played with complete freedom again in Jamaica, taking the fight to us and helped a little by Graham Dilley who bowled too wide of the off stump, hoping I suppose for an outside edge.

Larry Gomes, too, looked fairly comfortable, seldom in

trouble and an ideal partner while Clive was going so well. Larry is very much a one pace player, the reason why he was still 10 short of his century when the West Indies innings folded just before the close. Clive had failed to get his century too, just five runs short after 204 minutes at the crease with nineteen fours when he touched a delivery from Robin Jackman which bounced a little. It was a very thin edge and I doubt whether many in another large crowd realised he had touched it but Clive had no hesitation in walking without bothering to look at the umpire. The fact that 76 of his 95 runs were scored in boundaries underlines the power behind his innings.

I had one disappointment during the remainder of the West Indies innings — not being credited with a catch at silly mid-off against Malcolm Marshall when I dived to my left and held the ball just an inch off the ground. There was no doubt in my mind that the ball came off the bat rather than the pad. I stared at him. He stared back at me and made no effort to go. I was even more convinced I was right three balls later when he lifted John Emburey for six over wide mid-wicket which is usually a tell-tale sign the batsman is a little embarrassed. The next time he tried it against John, he was caught.

The rest day situation was an all too familiar one for us. No sun, of course with Ian Botham defiantly telling the cricket writers that he believed England could save it, Clive Lloyd insisting the wicket was beginning to behave mischievously enough for his bowlers to carry his side to another victory. From my point of view, I thought we could look back over the first three days with more to shout about than on any previous rest day of the tour. There was Graham Gooch's innings for a start, our ground fielding which I thought had been superb considering the roughness of the outfield which was like a minefield in places and also contained one area of concrete left over from all the rebuilding work and the emergence of Paul Downton as a wicket-keeper. He had been almost faultless, making a number of fine stops, particularly down the leg side, during the West Indies innings.

The only thing missing was a large contribution from myself and I did not have long to wait when the match started again with us 157 runs behind. We had wiped only five runs off when Graham Gooch fell to first slip against one from Malcolm Marshall which bounced more than he expected. We had scored only another five more when Bill Athey was caught behind against Michael Holding, an unfortunate dismissal. The ball was short and wide but did not bounce as much as he had expected and just flicked his glove.

That was the background to my entry. After telling myself in the morning that I was going to grab my final chance, I felt better walking to the wicket than I had done on any previous occasion on the tour. I didn't even feel that we were deep in trouble despite the reading on the scoreboard. No sooner had I got in than Marshall fed me one which went to the cover boundary right off the middle of the bat. Everything was right about the stroke. I felt at home, untroubled, even though I soon lost Geoff Boycott, caught in the gully off the glove against a Croft delivery which followed him as he tried to evade it. We were still 125 behind then but the sight of Peter Willey coming in gave me comfort.

He had not taken any nonsense from anybody on the tour. Tough, demanding and courageous in getting right behind the ball, rarely missing a chance to crack the ball to the boundary with the minimum fuss but maximum of muscle power. He made it easier for me because it is always better if there are two batsmen going together.

I still put up one black mark. I had enjoyed myself against Holding, a delivery which bounced high but I got intoposition quickly enough to give it a little help over the slips and the third man boundary for six. That made me feel even better. A minute later however I couldn't have felt worse. After that six Clive Lloyd had turned immediately to Viv Richards and I could have been out off the first ball. The ball was short and wide. I saw it as a four ball, one to have a go at and made the mistake of taking my eye off it at the last moment. I didn't connect properly but there was still sufficient contact to take Clive Lloyd by surprise at first slip.

From that moment onwards I can't recall being disturbed by anything else, not even the rain which interrupted the day and forced an early finish by which time I was on 70 and the partnership with Peter Willey with 102 which still left us needing another 23 to make the West Indies bat again.

Walking to the wicket the final morning was probably the worst moment of all. The century was so near, just 30 runs away. Yet it was still a long way off as I recalled the number of times I had been out for less than 30 during the series. Unfortunately I was to lose Peter Willey as my partner before I got there, Roland Butcher too.

Peter fell for the 'come on' ball from Viv, one tossed up asking to be hit. Peter went for it but not cleanly enough to be caught at wide midwicket to finish his contribution to the tour, a vital one all round. At the same score poor Roland was given out leg before when padding up and we were still in some danger when Ian Botham was caught in the gully. We were only 58 on and there was more than three hours to go. In addition West Indies had just taken the second new ball.

I had already scored my century by then, the magic moment coming when I swept Larry Gomes for four when Lloyd was employing an all spin attack to speed up the arrival of the new ball. For the chance to score the other 50, I was heavily indebted to Paul Downton. The West Indies realised that the second new ball presented their last real opportunity of making the breakthrough they wanted to clinch victory. Holding was extremely fast and nasty once more, showering Paul with a number of shortish deliveries when he first arrived at the crease but he got right behind every one.

We were not going to be completely safe until about half an hour after tea and it was more a question of giving it the grind over the final stretch of my innings. Paul did the same in staying three hours for his unbeaten 26. Throughout my partnerships with Peter Willey and Paul I had talked to them continuously and they had given me every encouragement. I had also spent almost two days talking to myself saying repeatedly 'come on, come on'.

At the end I was tired but happy in the knowledge that not only had I scored the runs I desperately needed but had done a good job at the same time. Perhaps the worst moment of all was facing up to the final ball from Gomes. I was worried it would get me out but I survived.

Throughout the tour people had commented that I had changed my style, I was no longer quite so risky outside the offstump, more selective in my strokes. Most of them put it down to my sacking from the England side after the Trent Bridge Test in England during the 1980 summer but I did not change overnight. I think I was helped last summer by playing on a number of wet wickets in the county championship, wickets on which scoring was difficult and I was forced to play a number of blocking type innings with scoring a secondary consideration. They helped to mould me, develop my concentration so that I was able to start the tour with an innings of seven hours fifty-five minutes and finish it with one just a couple of minutes longer.

I must give some credit to Peter Shilton, the England goalkeeper and an old acquaintance of mine. He called round at my Leicester flat shortly before the tour started and spelled out to me the need for self motivation, the necessity for getting away to a good start. I did -- and finished with one. I could sleep in peace on the final night. And I did.

WEST INDIES v. ENGLAND (Fifth Test)
JAMAICA, APRIL 10–15

England

G. A. Gooch	c Murray b Holding	153	c Lloyd b Marshall	3
G. Boycott	c Murray b Garner	40	c Garner b Croft	12
C.W.J. Athey	b Holding	3	c Murray b Holding	1
D.I. Gower	b Croft	22	not out	154
P. Willey	c Murray b Marshall	4	c Greenidge b Richards	67
R.O. Butcher	b Garner	32	lbw b Croft	0
*I. T. Botham	c Greenidge b Marshall	13	c Garner b Holding	16
+P.R. Downton	c Croft b Holding	0	not out	26
J.E. Emburey	b Holding	1		
R.D. Jackman	c Haynes b Holding	0		
G.R. Dilley	not out	1		
Extras	B 8, nb 8	16	B 6, lb 13, nb 4	23
Total		285	(6 wkts.)	302

Fall of wickets: 1—93, 2—148, 3—196, 4—210, 5—249, 6—275, 7—283, 8—283, 9—284.
1—5, 2—10, 3—32, 4—168, 5—168, 6—215

Bowling: First innings — Holding 18—3—56—5; Marshall 16—2—49—2; Croft 17—4—92—1; Garner 20—4—43—2; Richards 12—2—29—0.
Second innings — Holding 28—7—58—2; Marshall 5—0—15—1; Croft 29—7—80—2; Garner 24—7—46—0; Richards 23—8—48—1; Gomes 13—3—18—0; Mattis 5—1—10—0; Haynes 1—0—4—0.

West Indies

C. G. Greenidge	c Botham b Dilley	62
D. L. Haynes	b Willey	84
I. V. A. Richards	c Downton b Dilley	15
E. H. Mattis	c sub b Dilley	34
*C. H. Lloyd	c Downton b Jackman	95
H. A. Gomes	not out	90
+D. A. Murray	c Gooch b Emburey	14
M. D. Marshall	b Emburey	15
J. Garner	c sub b Dilley	19
M. A. Holding	c Downton b Botham	0
C. E. H. Croft	c sub b Botham	0
Extras	lb 8, w 1, nb 5	14
Total		442

Fall of wickets: 1—116, 2—136, 3—179, 4—227, 5—345, 6—372, 7—415, 8—441, 9—442

Bowling: Dilley 29.4—6—116—4; Botham 26.1—9—73—2; Jackman 26.2—6—57—1; Gooch 8—3—20—0; Emburey 56—23—108—2; Willey 18—3—54—1.

* captain + wicket-keeper

Match drawn

Averages

Batting

	M.	*Inns*	*Nos*	*Runs*	*H.S.*	*Average*	*100s*	*50s*
G. A. Gooch	4	8		460	153	57.50	2	1
D. I. Gower	4	8	1	376	154*	53.71	1	1
P. Willey	4	8	3	244	102	48.40	1	1
G. Boycott	4	8	1	295	104*	42.14	1	1
R. O. Butcher	3	5		71	32	14.20		
P. R. Downton	3	5	1	48	26*	12.00		
I. T. Botham	4	7		73	26	10.42		
J. E. Emburey	4	6	1	38	17*	7.60		
R. D. Jackman	2	3		14	7	4.66		
G. R. Dilley	4	6	3	11	7*	3.66		
C. W. J. Athey	2	4		7	3	1.75		

Played in one Test — B. C. Rose 10 & 5; M. W. Gatting 2 & 0; D. L. Bairstow 0 & 2; G. Miller 3 & 8; C. M. Old 1 & 0; G. B. Stevenson 1.

Bowling

	Overs	*Mdns.*	*Runs*	*Wkts.*	*Average*	*Best*	*5/inn*
I. T. Botham	145.2	31	492	15	32.80	4/77	
R. D. Jackman	73.2	15	198	6	33.00	3/65	
G. R. Dilley	130.4	25	450	10	45.00	4/116	
J. E. Emburey	185	62	419	7	59.86	5/124	1
P. Willey	47	12	111	1	111.00	1/54	

Also bowled: C. M. Old 16–3–49–1; G. Miller 18–4–42–1; G. B. Stevenson 33–5–111–3; G. Boycott 3–2–5–0 (all bowled in one Test); G. A. Gooch 14–5–36–0 (four Tests).

Catches

6 — P. R. Downton and D. L. Bairstow (inc. one as sub);
5 — I. T. Botham; 3 — R. O. Butcher, G. A. Gooch and M. W. Gatting (inc. two as sub); 2 — D. I. Gower, J. E. Emburey and G. Boycott;
1 — G. Miller and C. W. J. Athey.